M000211065

Social Media
Just for
Writers

Other books by Frances Caballo

Avoid Social Media Time Suck:
A Blueprint for Writers to Create Online Buzz for Their Books and
Still Have Time to Write

Blogging Just for Writers

The Author's Guide to Goodreads:
How to Engage with Readers and Market Your Books

Social Media in 30 Minutes a Day
Social Media Marketing Strategies and Tips for Busy Authors

Books available on my website
www.SocialMediaJustforWriters.com

Twitter Just for Writers

Pinterest Just for Writers

Social Media Primer with Advanced Guidelines

Social Media Just for Writers

How to Build Your Online Platform and Find and Engage with Your Readers

Frances Caballo

ACT Communications
Santa Rosa, California

Copyright © 2016 by Frances Caballo

All rights reserved. No part of this publication may be reproduced, distributed, or transmitted in any form or by any means, without prior written permission. For permission requests, write to the publisher at the address below.

Frances Caballo
ACT Communications
PO Box 14354
Santa Rosa, CA 95402
www.SocialMediaJustforWriters.com

Cover design by Matt Hinrichs
Formatting by Marny K. Parkin

Social Media Just for Writers
How to Build Your Online Platform, Find Readers, and Sell Your Books

—2nd ed. 2016
—1st ed. 2013

ISBN 978-0-9855592-6-7 (paperback)
ISBN 978-0-9855592-7-4 (ebook)

www.SocialMediaJustforWriters.com

For Carmen Rodriguez,
who always believed in me.

Contents

Acknowledgments

I am grateful for my cover designer, Matt Hinrichs, and designer, Marny K. Parkin. Arlene Miller also assisted with different part of this book. I'd like to acknowledge my readers; where would I be without you?

Introduction

This handbook is for you. You've spent more days than you can count working on your novel, memoir, or anthology of poems. You wrote, rewrote, corrected, edited, developed new scenes, twisted the plot, and returned to make additional edits. Finally, your book was ready for the world to see.

You celebrated your achievement. You invited friends to your book launch, welcomed them with glasses of sparkling wine and cheese, and scheduled readings at local bookstores. Then you wondered, "How can I reach more readers?" Selling books to your friends, colleagues, and family members was easy, but how do you reach people you don't even know?

By promoting your book online with social media, you can sell your books up and down your state, across the nation, and to people you have no idea how to reach. How, you ask? This book will explore and explain strategies for maximizing your online sales efforts. As a bonus, in the last chapter you will find tips for offline promotion too.

By the time you finish reading this book, you will know how to:

- Use Facebook effectively and efficiently to market your book.

- Tap into Twitter to create your tribe.

- Use virtual pinboards to expand the reach of your brand.

- Be more successful at blogging so you can reach new readers.

- Use LinkedIn with renewed confidence.

- Get started on Tumblr, Instagram and Snapchat to reach younger audiences.

- Learn how to incorporate more visual marketing into your social media use.

I wrote this book because authors like you asked me to write it. Like you, they wanted to feel more grounded in social media, learn to spend their time more resourcefully, and discover some of the secrets to social media marketing. They wanted a handbook they could take home to use as a reference.

Social media is a dynamic field, and networks are constantly updating features to improve the user's experience. While writing this book, I frequently rewrote portions and updated my screenshots so that you would have the most recent and relevant information possible.

To keep informed of the newest updates to Facebook, LinkedIn, Twitter, and Pinterest, Instagram, Snapchat and Tumblr, and to learn about new social media channels as they surface, visit my blog and website at www.SocialMediaJustforWriters.com.

This edition of Social Media Just for Writers deleted the chapter on Google+ due to changes on the social media landscape including the number of people using that platform.

You are about to begin your social media marketing journey now. Enjoy your time meeting and engaging with your readers.

Chapter 1
Not Sure How to Approach Social Media? CARE about Your Readers

From caring comes courage.
Lao Tzu

Among all the rules you'll find online—the 80/20 rule (only 20% of your posts should be about your books or blog posts while 80% of your posts should contain content from other sources), the admonitions against using social media as a bullhorn, the warnings about over automating—there's also an unspoken tenet.

This tenet isn't a rule that comes up on the blogosphere. Instead, it's more of a system of approach and an acronym that I created while preparing for the San Francisco Writers Conference.

If you follow the approach I'm about to explain, you can be sure that the time you spend on social media will generate the type of engagement with readers that you want to have.

Once you start to use social media, be prepared to CARE about people. I know that it seems evident to care about people online but give me a moment to break down the acronym.

C—Communicate with your readers.

A—Answer your readers' questions.

R—Relate to your readers.

E—Educate with stellar content.

And most of all simply care about people.

Joanna Penn devised the term social karma. As she explains it, if you want book sales, buy books. If you want book reviews, write reviews for all of the books you read. If you want people to like your Facebook page or follow you on Twitter, like your readers' and friends' Facebook pages and follow them on Twitter.

Reciprocate actions. And just as you might offer money to a homeless stranger, smile at a person walking down the street, or invite a new family from your church over for tea or dinner, take the types of actions online that will help you to get to know the people who follow you and want to connect with you.

In other words, be kind online. Be inquisitive. Be responsive. Be open to meeting people and revealing parts of your life.

Let's look more closely at CARE.

Communicate with Your Readers

The most basic tenet of social media is the ability to socialize with others, whether they are your readers, colleagues, friends, or key influencers. You've read blog posts in which bloggers decry those individuals who use social media to communicate too frequently the beleaguered mantra, "Buy my book."

To use social media as a bullhorn to talk about your books, yourself, and your blog posts is the opposite of social media's basic premise: to socialize with others.

Whether we're discussing Twitter, LinkedIn, Facebook or any other social media network, to continuously tweet or post status updates about the availability of your book is a violation of the trust your readers place in you when they decide to follow you or like your Facebook page.

What can you do instead? Communicate with your readers, colleagues, and influencers. Share experiences. Ask questions. Learn about them. Follow them. Share a funny incident. Discuss a common frustration or even fear. Express gratitude.

In the examples below, Mary Mackey, a New York Times historical fiction and fantasy novelist, received a message from a new follower. See how she responded to the comment, even though it wasn't about her directly or any books she'd written.

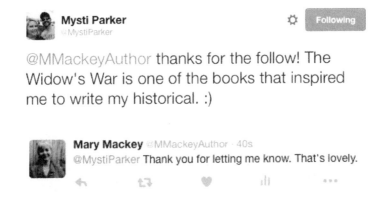

Answer Your Readers' Questions

How often do you respond to your readers' questions?

Make sure you're visiting your notifications, comments, and message areas across social media accounts checking to see if anyone is asking you a question—particularly on days when you're posting new content.

Sometimes, you won't find questions, but maybe a reader has left a comment that prompts you to ask a question. You won't know if you don't return to your posts.

The A in CARE is also for availability. Part of engaging with readers is being available to them online to address them one on one. Try to schedule 15 minutes every day to engage.

In this example, I answered a follower's question:

Relate to Your Readers

Do you really know your readers? You can become familiar with them by asking and answering questions and just talking with them on social media. That's right, have a conversation, even though the platform can be somewhat stilted it's still possible.

For example, I like to thank followers on Twitter for their retweets. On Facebook, I like readers' and friends' comments and if they leave a comment, I might have a follow-up question.

Another way to understand your readers and engage with them is to survey them periodically.

For example, after I'd been blogging for a while, I surveyed my blog readers, asking them to tell me what they most wanted to learn about in the future. I could have blindly decided on social media topics to write about, but engagement increases when I write about the issues already on the mind of my readers. You can do this either informally (through a social media or blog post) or formally, through a free Survey Monkey account.

Educate and Entertain

What do key influencers post on social media? If you study their posts you'll see that they tend to post a mix of tweets and updates that have excellent content and some entertainment value, whether it's in the form of quotes or memes.

For years, I've described Facebook as a balance of the mundane and the meaningful. I define mundane posts as entertaining and meaningful posts as those with an educational value. It's especially important to reach a balance between the mundane and the meaningful on Facebook pages.

If you look at my Facebook page, meaningful posts never receive as many comments, likes, or shares as entertaining status updates in the form of quotes and fun memes. But it's important to post links to valuable content for those fans that do value informative blog posts.

On Twitter, images always receive far more retweets than tweets without images. As a former vice president of Yahoo once told me, "Marketing is about entertaining." I choose to believe that I would have fewer followers if I didn't balance the entertaining tweets with valuable information that indie authors need to succeed in publishing and marketing. Marketing statistics back this up. It's common for visuals on Twitter to increase engagement by at least 25%.

The entertaining tweets and status updates are like the frosting on a cake, sugary sweet and fun to eat but what we really want is the cake, right?

Chapter 2
A Guide to Facebook

My wife, my family, my friends—they've all taught me things about
love and what that emotion really means.
In a nutshell, loving someone is about giving, not receiving.
Nicholas Sparks

If Facebook were a writer, the person penning the endless stream of romantic, tragic, and mundane status updates would be Nicholas Sparks. Sparks, author of more than a dozen books including *At First Sight, Message in a Bottle,* and *The Notebook,* is a prolific author who manages to always rank high on the *New York Times* Best Sellers List. His writing is approachable, and he has the ability to bring his readers to tears. You don't read Sparks to quench your literary thirst; however, you might grab his book off a rack right before boarding a flight to Greece because this writer knows how to spin a story.

Facebook is popular, approachable, and a fast, easy read. This social media behemoth is all about plot. People talk about book readings, family gatherings, their dogs and cats, and politics.

You, of course, will flit past the minutia of images of gluten-free hot dog buns and proud posts declaring, "I'm working out at 24-Hour Fitness right now!" and instead post real information. Perhaps you'll mention the literati you met at Book Expo America, the latest insight you gleaned from popular writer blogs, the book festival where you'll be a presenter, or a courageous new book a colleague published. The news can't always be about you, right? But your posts can and should be informative and interesting, like the first paragraph of a Wall Street Journal article. You want to write nuggets of great information that will leave your Facebook fans craving your next day's post.

Facebook Is Everywhere

Aside from the U.S. and Canada, Facebook is also popular in Germany, France, the Philippines, Turkey, the U.K., Mexico, Indonesia, India, and Brazil. In other words, it's popular around the world.

Some people enjoy complaining about how much they hate Facebook, yet despite many Internet users' love/hate relationship with Facebook there's no denying that it has still attracted 1.7 billion monthly active users and 1.4 daily active users.

Now for a Look at Facebook's Demographics

Consider these more concise facts from the Pew Research Center's Internet, Science & Tech Division. Their most recent report, **The Demographics of Social Media Users**, was published in November 2016 and provides further details about Facebook users.

- Facebook is used by 79% of all adult Internet users in the U.S.

- 83% of online female users are on Facebook.

- 88% of all online users between 18 and 29 are on Facebook.

- The United States is the largest market of Facebook users (14%), followed by India (14%) and Brazil (7%).

There's no denying that Facebook is widely used and that the majority of authors would benefit from having a profile and an author page.

Getting Started on Facebook

If you're new to Facebook, here's how to get started:

If you don't already have a Facebook profile, go to www.Facebook.com and open an account.

When you select your password, make sure it's hard to crack. Accounts on Facebook are hacked when passwords are weak so make sure that yours is a combination of upper and lower case letters, numbers, and symbols.

Upload an image of yourself for your avatar (the square profile picture or mug shot) as well as a cover image for your banner, which sits at the top of your Timeline. Don't forget to fully complete the About section.

Follow these photo dimensions:

- Profile image: 180 × 180 pixels

- Cover image: 828 × 315 pixels, and make sure it's a JPEG or PNG

For the Employment section, don't forget to include author as one of your job titles and include a link to your author website. When you designate your favorite books, don't forget to add books you and your colleagues wrote.

Facebook's Various Like Buttons

The Facebook Like button was updated with options in 2016. Users had clamored for a "dislike" icon for years. Facebook refused to give into that request and instead provided a variety of options. Instead of simply liking a status update, you can love it, laugh with your friends, or express your joy, sadness, or anger.

How to Switch Up Your Newsfeed

Do you want to switch the order of the posts that appear in your Facebook profile newsfeed (Home tab)? There are two ways to accomplish this. One way is to click on the arrow on your Facebook profile taskbar and select News Feed Preferences. Or you can navigate to your Home page (news feed) and click the arrow to the right of News Feed right below Favorites. See the screenshots here.

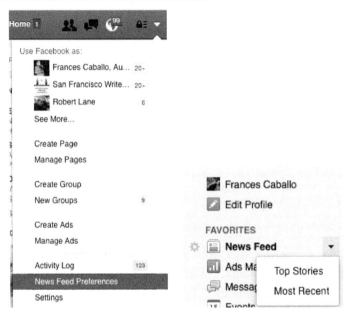

Sometimes when you like a Facebook author page or business page you don't see that author's posts in your news feed. Here's how to fix that. Navigate to that author's page, click the arrow next to Liked, and make your selection. First, under News Feed click a box.

Choose What You See from this Page

News Feed	Choose how you'll see Posts from this Page in your News Feed.
Notifications	**See First** See new posts from this Page at the top of your News Feed.
	• **Default** See posts in their usual order from this Page.
	Unfollow Never see posts from this Page in your News Feed.

Then, under notifications, make additional decisions.

Choose What You See from this Page

News Feed   Choose what types of post you want to be notified about.

Notifications   **Posts**
Get notified when this Page posts something new, which is about 8 times a
week. You won't see more than 5 notifications a day.

      All Posts

        Videos

        Photos

        Links

        Status Updates

Events Near You
Get notified when this Page hosts an event near you.

      Events

A Few Words about Safety and Facebook's Security Settings

Facebook can be fabulous for your author platform and help you communicate with your readers in a way that can rival other social media platforms.

As with all social media, it's important that you feel safe while using Facebook.

Here are some sobering facts about Facebook from HaltAbuse.org.

- The #1 location in the United States for victims and harassers is California.

- Most victims tend to be in the 18–40-year-old age group.

- Women are cyberstalked at a rate of 60%, compared to men at 40%.

- Harassment usually begins with email and escalates first on Facebook.

- Threats of offline violence occur in 25% of the cases.

National figures indicate that most stalkers are male by overwhelming margins (87 percent.) Men represented over 40 percent of stalking victims in the Penn-Rutgers study.

One of Facebook's Best Moves Ever— $1 for Your Thoughts

If you aren't friends with another person, you may be charged $1 if you want to send that Facebook user a private message.

Many women hailed this move when Facebook introduced it. Prior to implementing the charge, anyone could send a private, personal message to any user. Unfortunately, men who didn't know their female targets sent the majority of these private messages.

Some people still slip through the system. How? They send you a friend request and when you check out the person you might see that a friend of yours is a friend of this person who wants to become Facebook friends. You accept the friend request and then the inappropriate private messages begin.

What do you do? I block these types of individuals. Who wants to bother with an inappropriate spammer?

You can find private messages your friends sent you by clicking on the speech balloon or icon in your taskbar. It's located to the right of your friend requests. You can find private messages sent by Facebook users who aren't friends with you on the tab labeled Message Requests.

Facebook's Privacy Checkup Shortcut

If you navigate to your profile and look at the top blue taskbar, on the right you'll see a lock. This icon is your shortcut to your privacy settings.

"Who can see my stuff?"— When you click on this tab, you'll see this drop-down menu:

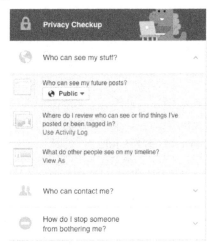

In this example, posts are set to Public. If you want to share your blog posts and other items on occasion from your author page to your profile, you may want to keep this setting on Public. If you are a sexual or domestic abuse survivor, you'll want to be more restrictive with this setting.

"Where do I review . . ."—This tab simply indicates which posts you've Liked and commented on.

"What do other people see on my timeline?"—This setting will remind you whether you allow future friends to see all of your posts or whether you hide your Timeline posts from "nonfriends." If you're not overly personal on Facebook, you may want to emulate the above example. If you keep your profile strictly personal and communicate only with trusted friends and family members, you'll need to be more restrictive.

"Who can contact me?"—Okay, this is where I recommend getting strict.

I accept private messages only from friends. And I like it that way. I'm also strict about friend requests. If you want to expand your platform on Facebook, you'll want to liberalize these settings.

I used to have liberal settings until people spammed my Timeline with announcements about their books, bras, and inappropriate images that they tagged me in. That's why I now have stricter settings.

I work on expanding my platform on other social media networks and keep strict settings on Facebook. But everyone's comfort level is different, and you need to decide what you're comfortable with.

"How do I stop someone from bothering me?" — You can block people easily. Just enter the name in the box, and he or she can't ever contact you on Facebook (unless you unblock them).

You can block someone to unfriend them and prevent them from starting conversations with you or seeing things you post on your timeline. [?]

Add name or email

View All Blocked Users

If You Want to Dig Deeper into
Your Facebook Privacy Settings . . .

After you click the lock in the taskbar, you'll see this message at the bottom of the first drop-down box: "See More Settings or visit Privacy Basics." Click on See More Settings and you'll arrive at this page:

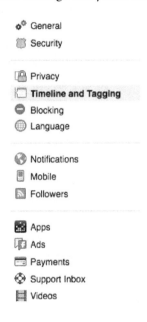

Timeline and Tagging Settings

Who can add things to my timeline?	Who can post on your timeline?	Friends	Edit
	Review posts friends tag you in before they appear on your timeline?	On	Edit
Who can see things on my timeline?	Review what other people see on your timeline		View As
	Who can see posts you've been tagged in on your timeline?	Only Me	Edit
	Who can see what others post on your timeline?	Only Me	Edit
How can I manage tags people add and tagging suggestions?	Review tags people add to your own posts before the tags appear on Facebook?	On	Edit
	When you're tagged in a post, who do you want to add to the audience if they aren't already in it?	Only Me	Edit
	Who sees tag suggestions when photos that look like you are uploaded?	No One	Edit

Let's look at the settings under Timeline and Tagging. You'll see that this is where I'm strict as well.

I like to see what friends want to post on my Timeline before it's published there. I also like to have some control over images I'm tagged in. Let's face it, I'm not photogenic, and I'm careful about my brand. It's important to me that everything on the Internet represents my author brand.

Under Blocking, you can block other users, app invites, event invites, applications, and pages. For a while I was receiving too many invitations to games that I don't have time to play. So I simply blocked the invitations:

Once you block an app, it can no longer contact you or get non-public information about you through Facebook. **Learn more**.

Block apps   [Type the name of an app...]

- BranchOut Unblock
- FarmVille Unblock
- Words With Friends Unblock
- Pillow Fight Unblock
- Birthdays Unblock
- Deep Sea Bubbles Unblock
- CityVille Unblock
- Bejeweled Blitz Unblock
- Ravenskye City Unblock

Social media is wonderful, but it's important that you feel safe while representing your brand and promoting your books. For additional information about controlling your privacy, visit this Facebook page: https://www.facebook.com/help/325807937506242/

Chapter 3
Facebook Author Pages—
All the Ins and Outs

How to Build Your Facebook Author Page

Let's start with a clarification: Facebook *profiles* are for people. In other words, you can send and receive friend requests and you'll interact with your friends, colleagues, and family members on a more personal note.

Facebook *pages* are for authors, artists, musicians, nonprofits, and businesses. You can Like other pages, but you can't send or receive friend requests. Your readers will Like your page and become your Facebook fans.

To create an author page, start by clicking the arrow in the upper blue Facebook taskbar and click on Create Page. Select the "Artist, Band or Public Figure" category, and then select Author in the options.

When designating a page name in the next option, use your name followed by a comma and the word *author* to differentiate your author page from your profile. (If you use a pen name, use that one instead.) This way, when someone searches for your name on Facebook, there will be two options:

1. Frances Caballo

2. Frances Caballo, Author

Similar to your Facebook profile, Facebook will prompt you to complete the About section, using 155 characters or less.

You'll also need to configure your Facebook web address for this page. You'll want it to be www.Facebook.com/YourNameAuthor

Next, upload a picture of yourself. Don't use your book cover or a picture of your dog/cat/canary. Your readers want to know what you look like so give them the pleasure.

The next step is to add your new Facebook page to your list of favorite pages.

Facebook Advertising

The next step in setting up your page will prepare you to purchase advertising in the future. You can elect to skip this section or complete it. I suggest that you complete this section.

Don't dismiss this part as unnecessary. Here's why: Several years ago, Facebook fans were able to see more than 30 percent of a Facebook page's status updates in their news feeds.

In the summer of 2014, Facebook adjusted its algorithm, dropping the visibility of Facebook author page posts to 6% to 12%. One year later, Facebook tweaked its algorithm again. The result? Unless your readers routinely Like, share, and comment on your updates, they will see only 2% of the updates you write.

To supersede that low percentage of views, you'll need to purchase Facebook advertising once in a while. Don't randomly promote posts; buy advertising when there's a clear call to action to purchase a book, grow your email list, or buy a service, and lead your readers to a designated landing page.

If you're a historical romance author, here is an example of how you might complete this Preferred Page Audience section. *Please note: Facebook has a large number of genres and interests in its database. The image merely serves as an example. The options will vary according to your genre. Please note that there are various types of ads, and this is just one example. Facebook advertising can be complex. For advanced training, visit Jon Loomer's website at http://www.jonloomer.com.*

Liking Your Page Isn't Vain

Next, Facebook will prompt you to Like your page. Do this. That way when someone visits your page soon after you create it, there will already be one Like.

Also, if you designate someone to help you with your page, that person will need to Like your page before you can add that individual as an Administrator of your page or as an Editor.

Brand Your Banner

It's time to create a cover image for the top of your author page. Go to Canva.com, a free application, sign up with an email and password, and select the Facebook banner template from the many options. Note: The correct image dimensions are built into the templates.

On Canva, you can select a template, search for appropriate images, upload the covers of your books, add the perfect background color to match your brand, and find your favorite font. There are numerous free templates on this website, and Canva is amazingly easy to use.

To learn more about Canva, check out its free tutorials: https://designschool.canva.com/tutorials/

A benefit of using Canva is that it incorporates into its templates every dimension you'll need for your social media images, and Canva updates those dimensions as the sizes change.

Once you create your cover, click the camera that says "change cover" in the lower, right-hand corner, and upload your new image. The camera icon will be a light gray, but will turn black when you hover over it.

Now you're ready to complete the About section and finalize your page information. Click About to the left of your Page's cover photo and beneath your avatar.

Frances
Caballo, Author
@FrancesCaballoAuthor

Home

| About

As you complete this section, think about your keywords and follow these steps:

1. Facebook will prompt you to enter your physical address and email address. Do you want people to know where you live? Probably not. Refrain from entering your email address in this section as well, or you might receive spam. Do you want to enter your phone number? Remember every detail entered in this section becomes visible to your readers and page visitors. How visible do you want your private information?

2. You have the option to enter your impressum, the statement of authorship or copyright on the front of your books.

3. Facebook will prompt you to write a long description. Make sure the description reflects your brand and includes your keywords. Despite Facebook's prompt to make this section lengthy, be concise. Few people will read a lengthy description.

4. Complete your bio.

5. Enter awards you've received.

6. List your favorite books. If you want others to read your books and designate them as favorites, you also need to show that you're an avid reader. This would be a good spot to list books that your colleagues have written too.

7. Add your website URL.

Insights: Facebook's Analytics Program

Once you have 35 page Likes, you'll need to check Insights, Facebook's free analytics program. Insights contains extensive data on your reader demographics, and this tool will help you learn which content resonates most with your readers.

Insights will also help you to determine when your ideal posting times are. Also, you'll learn about your page's newest Likes, "Unlikes," and the number of people your posts reach.

As one example, the graph below indicates the days and times when the fans in this example are on Facebook.

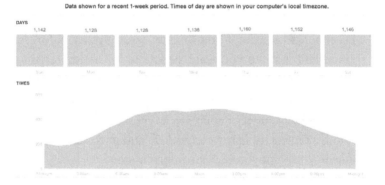

Don't Bother with Like Envy

Would you love to have a high number of page Likes? Here are a few tips:

1. Purchase advertising. When crafted correctly, it really works.

2. Add a personal touch to your page. Personalizing information from time to time will improve engagement and help your numbers multiply.

3. Use images and videos liberally.

Remember this: social media isn't a numbers game. It's never about how many followers you have or how many readers Like your page.

Social media is about engagement, and engagement is what Facebook's algorithm rewards.

You will invariably see ads online that encourage you to purchase Facebook Likes. Resist the temptation. Purchased Likes will adversely affect your analytics and will be apparent to anyone who visits your page. How? For example, when an author has 5,500 page Likes but only 11 people interact with a post, it's obvious that the author succumbed and purchased page Likes. Don't do it.

Grow your page organically, even though it will take time, by providing the type of content that will keep your readers returning. And periodically purchase an ad. This is the only true formula for success.

Do Authors Need a Facebook Page?

Do you need a Facebook author page?

Before I answer that question, let me distinguish a Facebook profile from a Facebook page.

On a Facebook profile, you have friends who share memes and information about their children, grandchildren, marathons, and other life events. And you can send and receive friend requests to and from anyone.

A Facebook page is for authors, musicians, nonprofits, large companies, and small businesses. You'll have fans instead of friends, and people and other pages will Like your page instead of sending you friend requests.

Here are some reasons why an author might need a Facebook page:

- Facebook doesn't allow the owners of Facebook profiles to market products and services. Profiles are designed as a means to exchange news with your friends and family members.

- If you want to purchase advertising to promote your books, services, and other products, you'll need a page. You can't buy advertising with a profile.

- A Facebook author page gives you the opportunity to focus on your readers, engage with your readers, and get to know your readers.

- Your friends might not want to hear about your books, services, blog posts, or other writing-related memes and status updates. Your readers will enjoy reading these items.

- Pages have access to Insights, Facebook's free analytics that can help direct the future success of your posts while providing valuable information about your fans' demographics and best times to post.

Now, here's a big reason why you might not want a Facebook page: Facebook's latest algorithm tweaks make it impossible for a typical indie author to have a successful Facebook page. One of the best ways to attract more clicks and fans is by purchasing advertising. But as I mentioned earlier, while others worry about high Like counts, you can focus on getting to know the readers who do Like your page and interact every day with the posts you add.

Facebook surveyed its users before instituting the latest changes to its algorithm and they discovered that people with profiles aren't so interested in hearing from business pages after all. But that's exactly what a Facebook author page is for. Facebook users actually prefer to hear from their friends, family members, and colleagues. So if you want to penetrate your readers' news feeds with your pithy posts, you're going to need to pay the piper, aka Facebook.

What Do Other Experts Say?

Industry experts are mixed in their opinions about Facebook pages. Jane Friedman doesn't have one and changed her hardline against Facebook pages recently. She wrote two posts on the topic. Her most recent one was in 2016 and titled "The Pros and Cons of Using a Facebook Profile But Not an Official Page," which I suggest you read.

Nathan Bransford believes that every author should have a Facebook page. Then there are those authors who mistakenly believe that they need a Facebook page for every book they write. Not so.

Multiple Facebook pages divide your audience and cause you to spend too much time managing them. Wouldn't you rather spend that time writing your next book? Let's examine this concept more closely. If you are a romance author, and you only write romance novels, you need only one Facebook page, if any at all. If you are a book coach offering a variety of coaching programs, you need only one Facebook page.

Let's say that you wrote a young adult novel, and then you wrote a memoir about battling cancer. Do you need two Facebook pages? You might. However, I think it's fine for your audience to learn that you write in two genres even if the audiences are distinct. If your readers feel connected to you, then they very likely would be interested in reading your memoir. This cross-pollination could work in your favor. Someone who only knows you as a memoirist might discover your YA books on your Facebook page, and vice versa.

There's another reason. YA readers can be diverse. Plenty of librarians and teachers like and read this genre. And some parents like to read them to keep up with what their kids are diving into. So not all YA readers are young and avid users of Snapchat.

But then again, some authors are shying away from Facebook pages and starting groups for their readers. I love this idea. So if you don't want a Facebook page but you do want deeper interactions with your readers on Facebook, opt instead for a Facebook group.

To create a Facebook group, follow these steps:

- Go to your "home page" (aka news feed) on Facebook.
- Then go to the Groups section on the grey, left-hand menu & find "+ Create Group".
- Facebook will prompt you to name your group, add people, and decide whether the group will be closed or open.
- Click Create.
- Choose an Icon.
- Complete "About" Section.

Convert Your Profile into a Facebook Page

A new feature from Facebook is the ability to convert a Facebook profile into a Facebook page. Here's how you can do it:

- Go to Create a Facebook Page Based on Your Profile by navigating to this link: https://www.facebook.com/pages/create/migrate

- Click Get Started and follow the on-screen instructions

Note:

- You can only convert your profile to a Page once.

- You'll still have a profile account as well as a Page once the conversion is completed.

- The tools to help you move information from your profile to your Page will only be available for 14 days.

- Posts from your profile won't carry over to your new page.

Are You Using Facebook Live?

Live streaming—broadcasting live from applications such as Twitter's Periscope—have grown in popularity in recent years. Facebook has it's own well tested live broadcasting native application called Facebook Live.

Let's examine how you can get started. Live is available to all pages and profiles and can be used on your mobile Apple and Android smartphones. Notice the word mobile. You can live stream on your iPhone or Android but you can't from your desktop computer.

When streaming a live video, the video will appear in your friends or fans' news feeds (Home tab), depending on whether you decide to stream from your Facebook profile or author page.

If you record from your Facebook profile, you won't have the option to edit the video. However, if you record using your Facebook author page, you can customize the video, which can be fun but will entail more time.

To make sure that your friends or fans can easily tune into your live video in the future, ask them to tap the "Live Subscribe" button on the top of a live video while streaming.

Why would you want to use Facebook Live? Jane Friedman uses Facebook Live to conduct "office visits." During the broadcasts, her Facebook friends can ask her any question they'd like about the publishing and book marketing industry.

You could use Facebook Live to connect with your readers. Think about how much fun it would be to give them an opportunity to ask questions with the author of books that they love to read. It's an exciting option for authors.

How to Start Using Facebook Live

To start broadcasting, tap the status update box on your mobile phone as though you were preparing to write a new Facebook post. In the vertical line of icons at the bottom of the status update box, you'll see a red icon. That's your Live button.

The next step is to tap Live Video and start recording. You're live!

Tools You'll Need

You can purchase expensive equipment or you can start with what you have on hand. Here's an overview of what you'll want to consider using once you're ready to purchase equipment.

1. Start with your iPhone or Android. Tap Live and start speaking into your phone.

2. If you don't think you can hold your phone steady, then invest in a tripod. You can spend about $50 for a Manfrotto tripod or spend $20 to $40 on a JOBY Gorillapod Flexible tripod.

3. Here again, you can use the lenses on your smartphone or purchase one. An example of one would be the Olloclip 4-IN-1 for the iPhone. Lenses on Amazon start at about $15.

4. Is the lighting good where you're shooting your video? If you're outside or near a window, the lighting should be fine. If you need

additional lighting, you could always purchase the Lumimuse 6 LED light for about $90.

5. Some people find that the mics on their smartphones aren't sufficient. If that's the case with your phone, consider purchasing the Rode VideoMic Me Directional Microphone for about $60.

Facebook Instant Articles

Instant Articles is another new mobile feature on Facebook, however, it's only available to users who have a Facebook page. To sign up, go to this link: instantarticles.fb.com.

Instant articles can breathe new life into your blog posts. Somewhat similar to LinkedIn's publishing platform, you can add your blog posts to Instant Articles. They, in turn, will load and display, according to Facebook, 10 times faster than a regular web page.

In addition, Facebook claims that:

- 20% more people read articles through this feature

- 70% of users are less likely to abandon an article or post

Here are some additional facts:

- Readers can identify an Instant Article because when it appears in your readers' (Facebook fans') news feeds, and it will have a lightning bolt icon.

- You can include videos in your articles.

- Your readers can share their thoughts, similar to the comments feature on your blog.

- You can link ads to your Instant Articles.

You aren't limited to adding your blog posts to Instant Articles. Authors can share the first chapter of a new book, poems, short stories, or news they want to share.

There is a caveat. In order for the content to load on this app, the story or blog post that you're trying to add must also be available on your website. Here is Facebook's explanation: "Having a standard web

URL that links to a web-based version of the content ensures that shared links to Instant Articles discovered on Facebook remain accessible to any reader on any platform."

The cool thing about Instant Articles is that after you've set everything up, and assuming that you'll add your blog posts to Instant Articles, you can automate the display of your content from your website to Facebook. But don't expect to be able to set up Instant Articles on your own. Your webmaster will need to add a meta tag to your HTML <head> tag and specify the URL (Internet link) you want to connect to Instant Articles and automate them.

There's more, too. Facebook offers content analytics for Instant Articles. The analytics include age, gender, language, and traffic data.

Instant Articles were originally set up for news organizations and big brands but there's no reason why indie authors can't enjoy the new feature as well.

Use Facebook's Scheduling Feature to Improve Engagement

As I mentioned earlier, avoid using a WordPress plugin that will automatically add a status update to your Facebook author page whenever you publish a new blog post. A better strategy is to go to your blog, click the social share button for Facebook, and write your status update.

Another alternative is to use Facebook's native scheduling feature located within the status update box. Once you add a few words, click the arrow to the right of the Publish button. Select schedule and then select the publishing date and time.

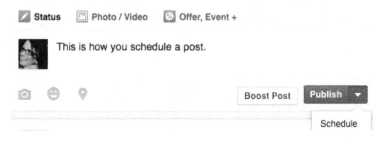

Schedule Post   ✕

Select a date and time in the future for when you
want your post to publish.

10/31/2015   🔲   1:07 PM   PDT

◀		October 2015			▶		**Schedule**
Sun	Mon	Tue	Wed	Thu	Fri	Sat	
				1	2	3	
4	5	6	7	8	9	10	
11	12	13	14	15	16	17	
18	19	20	21	22	23	24	
25	26	27	28	29	**30**	**31**	w at 9:18am. S

Facebook allows users to pre-schedule posts as far in advance as six months.

Facebook Page Best Practices & Tips

Engagement on Facebook is the key to Facebook's algorithm.

The algorithm, in basic terms, measures Likes, comments, and shares. Facebook shares are valued over comments and likes. What this means is that you need to create or find and post content that your readers regularly Like and share and comment on.

Your No. 1 goal will be to get your fans to share your status updates. Here are some general best practices and tips to help you along the way.

- Use only your best and most compelling images and most captivating, short (maximum of 90 seconds) videos. Images are important, but they won't trigger engagement with your readers unless they catch their attention.

- Post when engagement occurs, normally from 10 a.m. to 4 p.m. (Follow your time zone and the time zones of your readers. Always rely on Facebook's Insights as the final guide on this point.)

- Don't forget to post on the weekends when people have more leisure time to peruse their Facebook accounts.

- Keep your posts to 80 characters to encourage engagement. Readers like to move quickly through their news feeds.

- Don't ask your fans to Like or read your posts. Facebook will downgrade the visibility of your status update if you include this type of call to action.

- Respond as soon as you can to queries and concerns your readers post on your Timeline and private messages sent to you.

- Try to post twice daily on your fan page.

- Host contests. Use RaffleCopter to keep track of entries.

- Promote your colleagues, and if your readers write books, help them as well.

- Share blog posts you write, but don't auto-post from your website. When you use a WordPress plugin that automatically generates a status update each time you publish a post, Facebook will downgrade the post and few of your readers will see it. Instead, use the social share icon on your blog.

- Share blog posts that others write if the information is relevant to your readers.

- Offer a chapter of your book for free. Post it on Scribd, GoodReads, or your website and provide a link to the chapter on Facebook.

- Schedule time to socialize on Facebook. Read your readers' status updates, and leave Likes and comments or share their posts.

- Vary your content. For example, ask your readers what they are reading or how they plan to spend the weekend.

- Seek your readers' help by asking them to suggest names for your characters in a new book you're writing. Or ask them to help you select a book cover. Involve your readers as much as you can in the creation of your books.

- Tag your Facebook fans in photos you post on your page and in replies to their comments.

- Allocate resources to Facebook advertising, even if you spend $5/day. Ads on Facebook can increase the visibility of your fan page and help you to reach new readers.

- Remember to like your readers' fan pages, if they have them, and leave comments or share their content when relevant.

- Join a Facebook group some of your readers may belong to provided the topic is of interest to you.

- Regularly review your Facebook Insights looking for trends, identifying drops in fan engagement, and analyzing posts that triggered the most Likes and comments.

- Mix up the days and times you post on Facebook. You'll, of course, want to check your Insights to see when your fans are on Facebook. But you'll also want to check for when they are most likely to engage, and the only method to find that out is by mixing it up.

- Include some personality. People do not buy books from brands; they buy books from writers, so don't be afraid to share information that reveals more of your personality.

- Don't be afraid to take a stand on an issue in your niche, genre, or recent events.

- Vary your types of posts. Vary the topics, the length, the types of images you use, and the types of questions you pose.

- Consider freshening up your cover image on a quarterly basis using Canva or PicMonkey.

- Host a Facebook Friday networking party that enables your readers to promote their books, blog posts, or other types of news. Get to know your readers and what matters to them.

- Drive traffic from other social media sites to posts you want to receive additional attention. This is how: When you click on the date stamp of your Facebook post, you'll see that your post has a unique URL. You can drive traffic to that post by using that URL in a tweet or LinkedIn post. Here is a post in a timeline; the date stamp is November 2 at 11:20 a.m.

 Frances Caballo, Author
November 2 at 11:20am · Edited [?] ·

I've never actually said this to anyone. Have you?

341 people reached   Boost Post

Next, click on the date stamp. The date stamp in the above images is November 2 at 11:20 am. The web address at the top of the page has a unique address. In this case, it's https://www.facebook.com/Frances CaballoAuthor/photos/a.364295866972899.81420.362213273847825/9134 40035391810/?type=3&theater.

When you tweet the above URL, your followers will see the image and all of the comments beneath it:

Use this strategy to drive more traffic to important or popular Facebook posts to drive even more engagement.

9 More Tips to Attract Readers to
Your Facebook Author Page

Want your readers to show up more frequently and share your content? Here are some tips:

1. Invite your Facebook friends and other followers and connections to visit your Facebook page by posting content that links to your Facebook page.

2. Consider adding a Facebook Like Box to your website.

3. Cover the basics. Complete the About section, upload a branded banner image, and use a picture of yourself that projects the image of a professional.

4. The next time you prepare an e-newsletter, remember to include a Facebook social share icon and Like icon.

5. Add a link to your email signature that leads readers to your Facebook page.

6. Include a call to action at the end of each of your blog posts encouraging your readers to Like your Facebook page.

7. Include your Facebook page URL on your business card and the back cover of your book.

8. When you leave a comment on a blog, consider leaving the web address for your Facebook page instead of your website URL.

9. Remember to add your Facebook Author page web address on the bottom of all press releases.

Chapter 4
Your Complete Guide to Twitter

A poem begins as a lump in the throat,
a sense of wrong, a homesickness, a lovesickness.
Robert Frost

Twitter Is Its Own Universe—It's a Twitterverse

Twitter is tremendous. The 140-character limit to tweets can seem restrictive at first, but you'll find the limitation liberating. Think of Twitter as poetry. Henry James, with his long sentences, and Faulkner, who used adjectives profusely, would not have embraced Twitter. However, Miguel Hernández, the famous Spanish poet and anti-Fascist soldier of the Fifth Regiment during the Spanish Civil War, would have felt comfortable with it. Hernández wrote some of his poetry on slips of paper while fighting in the trenches. Similar to "retweeters," soldiers read and passed along the lines of poetry as they fought in the valleys and rested in the cafes of Spain. Each short stanza of a Hernández poem is perfect in itself, just like a carefully crafted brief Twitter post. Or in today's vernacular, just like an #Instapoet. (This term started on Instagram and refers to poets who share lines of their poetry as images. The hashtag is also used on Twitter.)

You threw me a lemon, so bitter,
with a hand warm and so pure,
that its shape was not spoiled,
and I tasted its bitterness regardless.
from You Threw Me a Lemon, El Rayo Que No Cesa

As the cultural affairs officer in the First Calvary Company of the Peasants' Battalion, Hernández organized poetry readings. He also joined the First Calvary Company of the Peasants' Battalion as a cultural-affairs officer, reading his poetry daily on the radio.

He traveled extensively throughout the area, organizing cultural events and doing poetry readings for soldiers on the front lines, or even pitching in where necessary to dig a ditch or defend a position. As more and more war poems flowed from his pen, he slowly approached the status of poet of the nation during the war years.

Twitter in the 21st Century

If you want the most up-to-date news you can find, you'll discover it on Twitter. If there's an earthquake in Mexico, Japan, or San Francisco, a user will report the first tremor. Protests in Libya, Tunisia, and Egypt have been called Twitter revolutions, and the social media channel has been credited with furthering causes.

Twitter is a happening place—and it's fun. Success on Twitter is determined by how social you are, how courteous you are, how informative you are, and how much you engage with the faces behind the avatars.

One of the beauties of Twitter is that it adheres to protocols that even Miss Manners would approve of. Users always acknowledge the original authors of tweets, which most often include links to blog posts on a range of topics, news items, or famous quotes. Miss Manners must also think highly of Twitter users who send thank-you messages to users who retweet (resend) messages or type a short note of encouragement or praise.

Some of the greatest minds in technology, publishing, writing, public relations, and other fields are on Twitter and they freely share their expertise with other professionals. This channel is probably the best platform to keep up to date on writing conferences, writing prompts, newly released books, social media, book marketing strategies, or whatever your fields of interest are. It's on this network where you can learn to publicize your book, find a publisher, seek an agent, find colleagues, or learn more about a certain genre.

One benefit of Twitter is that you'll see practically instant results. If you retweet someone's message, the likelihood is high the person will send you a thank-you tweet—immediately. If you ask a question, people will answer. If you have concerns or suggestions about an application, you can tweet the creator of the application. On Twitter, nearly everyone is accessible because that is the nature of Twitter. To be successful, all you have to do is make yourself available to your audience and get to know its members.

Twitter is the place to glean great gems of information, expand your contacts, and share your own expertise. There isn't another social media network like it—at least not yet. The limitation of 140 characters doesn't diminish the impact of this great social media channel. In fact, the Facebook posts that are most widely read are about 80 characters. In this era when the attention span of many people is shrinking, tweets are an efficient way to communicate great nuggets of information.

So sign up and get going. If you're social on Twitter, your tribe will form and grow. Just release the poet in you, become a trusted authority, meet new colleagues, find readers, and have a lot of fun.

How to Get Started on Twitter

Have you been ignoring Twitter? Do you think you don't have time for it? Twitter is an important social media network for Indie authors.

You already know that social media in general will help you to build your brand and connect with new readers. Well, Twitter, like no other social media network, will be especially helpful in connecting with readers around the globe. You'll also meet other Indie authors as well as publishing experts, agents, publishers, and accomplished bloggers within your niche and the publishing field in general.

Through Twitter I met a writer and blogger from Wales. As soon as my first book was published, he asked me to write a post for his blog. My book immediately started selling in the U.K. and did for years.

I'm active on other social media platforms, yet Twitter has created opportunities for me and is responsible for my book sales in nearly every pocket of the United States and in other parts of the English-speaking world.

Twitter can do the same for you and your books as well.

One benefit of Twitter is that you will see instant results. If you retweet someone's message, the likelihood is high the person will send you a thank-you tweet—immediately. If you ask a question, people will provide answers. On Twitter, everyone is accessible because that is the nature of Twitter.

Start with the Basics

If you are new to Twitter, here are some initial steps you'll need to take.

Sign Up

Navigate to Twitter.com and sign up by including your first and last names, phone or email address, and a password.

Create a Password That Can't Be Hacked

When you select your password, make sure it's impossible to crack. Use lowercase and uppercase letters, numbers, and symbols such as ^ or #. Do not use the word "password" in your login; there are 10 million people who already use it, so it's easy for hackers to guess.

Here's an easy system for creating passwords you'll never forget:

1. Write down the last names of your two favorite authors.

2. Use the first three letters of one of the author's last names to start your password. Let's say you selected Hemingway. The first part of your password would be Hem.

3. Select three or more numbers. Don't use 123. Mix the numbers up.

4. Use the first three letters of the second author's last name. Let's say it's Allende. So far your password might be Hem982All.

5. Add symbols to the mix. Your final password might be Hem9*82All@ or Hem982All*@.

6. As you add social media networks, change one variable. Now you'll have a unique password for each social media network you use.

To be safe online, create a unique password for every social media network, application, and email program you use.

Select a Username/Twitter Handle

Your next step is to decide on your username, also called a handle. Try to restrict your username to 12 characters or fewer, even though you're allowed 15. Brevity is important on Twitter where every character counts. Consider these tips before hitting save:

1. If possible, use your full name. In my case, @FrancesCaballo was taken by a Spanish soccer player, so I chose @CaballoFrances. This username preserves my identity and brand, even though it has 14 characters.

2. Do not add numbers to your username as in @DebSmith15. When people search for you on Twitter, all the other Debbie Smiths or Deborah Smiths or Deb Smiths will appear in the search results ahead of you, making it difficult for potential readers to find you. Potential followers might even start following the other D. Smiths simply because they trumped you in search results. Instead, try @DSmith or @DebbieS or even @SmithDeb.

3. Don't use spammy handles such as @LatteLover, @Smith_10, or @x43_107. These types of usernames will hamper your efforts to establish your brand and online visibility. *Final word on this topic:* Never use a number in your handle.

4. In some instances you can choose to be unique, but be careful with this. Linda Joy Myers, founder of a national organization

for memoir writers, is known as the Memoir Guru, so it makes sense that her handle is @MemoirGuru. Penny Sansevieri probably chose @Bookgal as her handle because people tend to have difficulty pronouncing or spelling her last name and because she is a book publicist. But note that there's also @thebookgal on Twitter; however this user has a following of only 14 followers compared to Penny's 37,000+ followers.

5. Don't use an underscore in your handle. First, it can be difficult to detect the underscore (_) symbol. Similar to numbers, underscores give the impression that you're late to the party, your preferred handle was taken, and that you didn't know what to do, so—perhaps in a hurry—you quickly tossed in an underscore. If you can't use your name because it's too long or it's already taken, consider the branding examples above, as demonstrated in @MemoirGuru and @Bookgal as well as Joel Friedlander's @JFbookman.

Write Your Bio

You have 160 characters to work with. Think about what you want your audience to know about you and how you can further your brand in 160 or fewer characters. If possible, include keywords and a link to your recently published book or Author Central page on Amazon. Here are some sample bios:

Joel Friedlander
Writers change the world one reader at a time. But you can't change the world with a book that's unpublished. Self-publishing puts your book in readers' hands.

Susanne Lakin
Author of 16 novels and 6 writing craft books. A writing coach, copyeditor and blogger @LiveWriteThrive. Get a free eBook for writers at http://www.LiveWriteThrive.com

Susanne's example of including a link to a giveaway document is an excellent strategy to emulate.

Isabel Allende
Cuenta cuentos, escritora, activista y bajita. | Storyteller, writer and activist; also known for being vertically challenged.

Note the use of both English and Spanish. This makes sense for Allende since she publishes in both languages.

Lisa Tener
Book writing coach, blogger, speaker. Helping experts + enlightened entrepreneurs write and publish. Get your complimentary author toolkit at LisaTener.com

Elizabeth S. Craig
Writes two mystery series for Penguin Random House and self-publishes another. Tweets writing links.

Tweet in 140 Characters or Less

Some authors are perplexed by the 140-character limit. Writers often ask, "What can I say in 140 characters?"

We fool ourselves if we think that our readers have the time or patience to read long social media posts. On Facebook, for example, recent studies indicate that the most successful status updates contain just 80 to 190 characters.

On Twitter, you can actually say a lot in 140 characters and even 120 characters, which will be your true character limit if you want your content to gain traction and spread through retweets. Why must you use just 120 characters? Because when people retweet you as they schedule their tweets, there won't be room to include your username in a retweet if you use up all of your allotted 140 characters.

However, if others tweet you live, meaning while they are on Twitter, you could use up the 140 characters. Why? Because live retweets—called Quote Tweets—look like this as you write them.

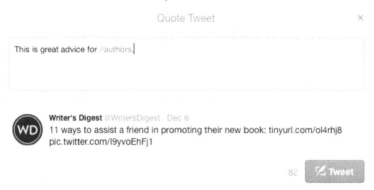

And this is how they appear in your stream.

Customize Your Image

Your next step will be to customize your profile. Click Edit Profile to upload your profile and header images. Click the camera in the header image area and upload your own image.

Your header image should be 1,500 × 500 pixels and can be a composite of your book titles or an image that reflects the theme of your book. In all of your images, consider how they further your brand.

Use Canva.com, a free online application, to create a unique header image as mentioned in Chapter 2.

Once you upload your images, click Save Changes.

Your profile image—also known as your avatar—will be a picture of you and needs to be 400 × 400 pixels.

To customize the color of your links and edit your bio and website link, click Edit Profile again. Be sure to select a color that's consistent with your brand.

Twitter's Tabs

It's time to familiarize yourself with Twitter's tabs.

Home
When you click on Home, you will arrive at your newsfeed where you can see a lengthy and fluctuating stream of incoming tweets. The newest updates will always appear at the top. Your Home Tab is your news feed; Facebook uses the same term.

Notifications
The Notifications tab will provide you with information about new followers, retweets, mentions, and likes, which are denoted by a heart that turns red once you click it.

Moments
Twitter uses this tab to keep its users up to date on the day's top stories. The network also provides separate tabs for stories that are newsworthy, important in sports, entertaining, and just fun. You'll also find trending hashtags and suggestions for whom to follow.

Messages
This tab provides a list of people who have sent you direct messages. Direct messages are visible only to the sender and the recipient of tweets.

Twitter's Gearshift

The Gearshift
You'll find a gearshift located to the left of the Follow button on profiles you visit. You won't find one on your profile.

Click the gearshift if you want to:

- Tweet to someone

- Send a direct message

- Add the follower to one of your lists

Are You Ready to Tweet?

When you're ready to tweet, click the quill pen to the right of your image on the upper taskbar. You can also use this feature to tweet images and tag other users in the images you send.

How to Access Lists, Analytics, Settings, and More

Click your profile image to the left of the quill pen in the taskbar to conduct a variety of activities.

- Create or access your lists

- Ask Twitter a question

- Access a list of keyboard shortcuts

- Create an ad

- Find your analytics

- Change your settings

- Log out

Never Do This on Twitter

Don't Text on Twitter

In the microblogging sphere, every character counts. When your ultimate limit is 140 characters, you have to kill every appearance of *the, but, or,* and similar extraneous words. Some users employ texting language (*I luv u* instead of *I love you*) in their tweets. Avoid doing this.

You're a writer and it's important to use correct spelling in your online messages.

Keep Your Links Tiny

If you post live on this platform, Twitter will automatically shorten a long link for you. If you instead use a social media dashboard to schedule your tweets for the day or the week, you need to shorten the link before saving your tweet. You may also use a URL shortener such as Bit.ly. For example, Bitly can shorten the link http://www.thebookdesigner.com/2014/07/ this-week-in-the-blogs-july-12-18-2014/ to bit.ly/1qUFixu.

Four Tweets You Should Never Send

- Stop sending tweets announcing how many people you followed or unfollowed using an application that accomplishes this task for you. These types of tweets do nothing to build your brand or following.

- Do not send direct messages to solicit the purchase of your books or to communicate information about your website or blog. In fact, don't send direct messages unless you're trying to contact someone you know to convey your email address or phone number or to thank them for referring a client to you.

- Think twice before sending someone a thank-you tweet just for following you. Your time could be better spent doing something else, such as writing a blog post, working on your next book, or finding content to retweet.

- Don't send a successive train of tweets in a row. It's not nice to flood someone's newsfeed with a day's worth of messages in the span of a few minutes. If you do this, you will lose followers.

15 Tips to Get You Started

Here are some quick tips on how to make the most of your time on Twitter.

1. Check the Notifications Tab daily, and respond to questions as promptly as you can. In addition, thank followers who retweet your content and images.

2. Tweet your blog posts. Use a variety of headlines, and test which headlines result in the most retweets and click-through rates to your website.

3. Tweet at least three to five times daily, and space your tweets throughout the day.

4. If you are running a contest on your Facebook page, let your Twitter followers know about it.

5. Share your e-newsletter on Twitter, and invite people to sign up.

6. Don't cross-post your Twitter content to Facebook and LinkedIn. You need to develop a distinctive voice on each network.

7. If you're conducting research for a blog post or book, ask your Twitter followers for their ideas.

8. Twitter has a limit on the "follow ratio" of its users. Once you reach 2,000 Twitter followers, Twitter will limit the number of users you follow to 10% more than the number of users following you. If you have 3,000 followers, you can follow only up to 3,300 users. Note: There's no limit on the number of followers you can have.

9. If someone tweets a compliment to you, do not retweet it. This is akin to laughing at your own jokes when no one else is.

10. Allocate time to be social on social media. Initiate conversations by asking questions, praising others, and following the 80/20 rule: 80% of the time, you promote others and 20% of the time you can promote your books and blog posts.

11. Thank people who spread the news about your books.

12. Retweet from a variety of sources. If you always tweet the same few sources, your tribe might not grow.

13. Help other writers promote their books. Join an online community such as Triberr to build your tribe, or get to know other writers by asking them questions.

14. Always credit the author of the content that you retweet.

15. Use an application, such as Tweepi or ManageFlitter, to unfollow spam and fraud accounts, and anyone you no longer wish to follow.

Why Twitter Is Awesome for Authors

Unconvinced that Twitter is for you? Here are some reasons why Twitter is awesome for writers.

- If you're active on Twitter, it will refer traffic to your blog and website.

- There is a large community of Indie authors on Twitter who will be eager to help you promote your book and form supportive alliances. Endeavor to meet other authors in your genre, share blog posts, and promote each other.

- Twitter will help you to market your books.

- Twitter is where the news happens. If you read newspapers or listen to the radio, your news is old. What happens around the world is reported first on Twitter. How does this help you as an author? As an online marketer, you need to stay abreast of the news to incorporate big stories in your posts. Who knows? Some events might even relate to your books. For example, if you write a young adult novel featuring a young, female athlete, you'd want to tweet about the Women's World Cup.

- You can use hashtags to easily find your readers, book bloggers, reviewers, and literary agents on Twitter. You can also use hashtags to find people who love to read.

- Who wants to write long updates after spending the morning writing your next chapter? Twitter is great because the platform limits you to just 140 characters, including spaces.

Twitter Demographics

We know that 23 percent of online adults living in the United States are active on Twitter. And thanks to the Pew Internet Research Project, we know several facts about these users. According to this study

- Among the 24% of online users who have accounts on Twitter, 32% are between 18 and 29 years of age. And 23% of them are between 30 and 49. Older demographics have significantly lower user rates.

- There are far more Hispanic and Black Twitter users than White users.

- The gender split tilts slightly in favor of females by 1%.

Interpreting the Research Results for Authors

What can we assume from these statistics? YA and New Adult writers need to have an active presence on Twitter. This is one of the places where your readers hang out, in addition to Instagram and Tumblr.

Authors who write in Spanish or who write novels based in Spanish-speaking countries would do well on Twitter. Also, authors who write books with African-American characters or historical accounts of the civil rights movement, slavery, and related issues, should use Twitter as well.

Does this mean that only authors of those genres or niches should use Twitter? No, but understand that the user base can influence your success on Twitter.

The final test in determining whether Twitter is appropriate for you is to simply try it. I'm of the belief that all authors should have Twitter accounts and maintain an active presence.

Twitter has thousands—if not hundreds of thousands—of avid readers looking for the next great book in their genre of choice. You'll also find editors and publishing experts on this platform as well as meet other authors with whom you can help market each other's books. And on Twitter, you'll have opportunities to meet, follow, and converse with the top industry experts. If you're an author, Twitter is indispensable.

Reorder Tweets in Your Newsfeed

In February 2016, Twitter introduced an algorithm to its news feed to resemble what Facebook uses.

Before you scream, the change doesn't exactly match what Facebook does. You, as the user, can decide whether you want to see "the best tweets first" from your followers and those you follow.

This is how Twitter introduced this concept on its blog:

"Here's how it works. You flip on the feature in your settings; then when you open Twitter after being away for a while, the Tweets you're most likely to care about will appear at the top of your timeline—still recent and in reverse chronological order. The rest of the Tweets will be displayed right underneath, also in reverse chronological order, as always."

If you want to keep your newsfeed free of any algorithmic tweaks, do nothing. If you want to turn on the change to see what it might be like, open your settings and choose "Show me the best tweets first." It's that simple.

Chapter 5
Applications Just for Twitter

I have a great support network—my family, my model agency Storm, and people I work with in the fashion industry. And, of course, there are all my followers on Twitter who stop me from feeling lonely; I love them all. They keep me grounded.
Cara Delevingne

You now know how to create your Twitter profile, and you have all of my best tips in your arsenal. It would be helpful to learn about the Twitter applications that can ease your tweeting and deepen your experience. I've tried all of the applications below.

Tools for Bouncing Unfollowers and Fraud Accounts

ManageFlitter
You can use the free version of this tool to unfollow a limited number of your Twitter followers who aren't following you. With the $12/month plan, you have access to additional features including finding and blocking fraud and spam accounts, and identifying which users you never want to unfollow. PowerPost is another paid feature. With PowerPost, ManageFlitter determines the best hour and day to send a power tweet.

Tweepi
This is a standard application that you can use for free—or pay to use—to clean up your Twitter account of users who don't follow you back.

The paid version allows you to designate influencers you want to keep in touch with and never unfollow. A paid account also allows you to block undesirable types, such as bots or spam accounts.

Unfollowers

You can use this app for Twitter and Instagram to unfollow anyone who isn't following you back. The free account limits the number of users you can unfollow each day.

Who Unfollowed Me?

With this application, you can track unfollowers, new followers, people you follow who don't follow back, and people who follow you whom you don't follow back. As soon as you sign up for this free app, it will generate this type of dashboard:

The Pro plan costs $9.99/year and offers additional features.

Apps with Analytics

Twitonomy

This app offers detailed, visual analytics on your Twitter users' tweets, retweets, replies, mentions, and hashtags. You can also export analytics, back up your tweets, monitor your interactions with your readers, download a copy of your followers, and track clicks from your tweets.

Followerwonk

Use this app to dig deeper into your Twitter analytics and to find and connect with influencers in your niche or genre. Followerwonk offers a free plan.

Daily 140

After you sign up for this app, Daily 140 will send you an email every day with information about several Twitter users you select to monitor. The information includes their new followers and tweets they've liked. Use this tool to monitor and learn from experts in your niche or field.

Riffle

Available in the Chrome Web Store, Riffle endeavors to teach you about your community on Twitter. Features include statistics, popular hashtags, and more. The app can help you find influential Twitter users too.

Stats for Twitter (& Instagram)

Made for Apple products, this app can monitor metrics, including retweets and faves. It also provides detailed graphics that detail your performance on Twitter.

Note: There are plenty of analytics tools that will provide detailed information. Examples of these are SpoutSocial (starts at $59/month) and Social Report (starts at $19/month, but better analytics are available for $49/month). Indie authors, however, can uncover analytics for free from most social media networks, including Facebook, Pinterest, and Twitter. Or you can use the free to low-cost apps detailed above. You can also upgrade to paid plans on scheduling applications, such as Hootsuite and SocialOomph, to gain access to analytics and information on click-through-rates (clicks on links that lead to your designated landing pages) for less money than many analytics programs.

Chat Apps

A Twitter chat is an online conversation that takes place on Twitter at a specific starting time. They typically last one hour.

Twubs

Once you sign up with Twubs, you can join chats, and the application will automatically add the chat hashtag to your tweets. You can even join Twitter chats right on the Twubs website. It's convenient and fast and keeps you updated with the latest addition to the conversation. A paid version allows you to create landing pages on Twubs for the chats you host.

TweetChat

To begin using TweetChat, simply type a hashtag. I used the hashtag #twitterchat and within two seconds TweetChat provided me with a stream of tweets using that hashtag. Right from this app, you can reply to real-time tweets during a live chat.

TwChat

This free app allows you to view real-time chats.

Cool Apps

Hibari

This app, which is a program you download, is for Mac users only. Once you download this tool, you can block tweets from users based on keywords, mute Tweeps you need to follow but whose tweets may be annoying, and highlight the type of information you want to find.

TweetCaster

This free app has many features, so I'll just highlight my favorites. You can use it to add captions that you upload to Twitter, and filter your tweets so you'll quickly find the nuggets you're looking for. Its "zip" feature deletes annoying tweets from your timeline. iPhone users can download it from the App Store. Android users can get it from GooglePlay.

Tweetings

This app is available for iPhone and Android users. Tweetings will create a map that shows where your Tweeps are from, and it will let you update your Twitter account. You can view your news feed in real time, view your Twitter lists, see who retweeted you, open links in the background so you don't lose your place, and more. You can also follow and unfollow users, manage unread tweets, post messages, and retweet.

Themeleon aka Colourlovers

Every Twitter account needs a professional-appearing background theme and header image. You can use this application to create a theme that matches your brand.

Bluenod

If you want to see schematics on your followers or on other Twitter users, you'll find them with the help of this application. The starting price is $29/month. However, I used to find it helpful for finding new followers.

Tweriod

Find the best time to tweet with this free application. Tweriod will analyze your tweets as well as your followers' tweets to find your optimal tweeting time.

Periscope

Live streaming is hot and with this Twitter app you can broadcast a program or tips session using your smartphone. Be sure to follow @AlexPettitt because he's an expert, one of the world's top three Periscope users, and he "scopes" often.

Hashtag Help

Tagboard

This is a useful app for determining if a hashtag you create is already taken and to define hashtags you may not understand. If you type in a hashtag, such as #amwriting, Tagboard will, within seconds, provide a visual map of the hashtag's use and include trending statistics.

Social Bearing

This application provides real-time Twitter searches, insights, and information on mentions and engagement. Actually, it provides even more information. In the example below, I used the hashtag #amwriting. See the results here:

Use the above applications to discover and join chats, discard unfollowers, and monitor aspects of your account. Apps can be fun to use, help you to save time, and deepen your Twitter experience.

Chapter 6
Hashtags and Terms for the Twitterverse

Whatever one thinks of Twitter,
the Friday Reads hashtag is kind of a cool tradition.
James Bernard Frost

Terms Every Writer Needs to Know

Every country has a language, and some even have a host of distinctive dialects. In the Twitterverse of social media, Twitter has a unique and expanding use of Twitter-specific terms. To help you keep up with the twists and turns of Twitterspeak, you can refer to two websites, Twictionary and Twittonary.com. Here's a list of terms to get you started.

- **DM:** This abbreviation stands for Direct Message. If you want to send a more private message to a reader or colleague, this is the function to use. Warning: Some writers use this feature to spam their followers with information about their books and blogs. Don't do this. How can you tell if someone has sent you a direct message? You'll see a number to the left of the word Messages in your Twitter taskbar.

- **Like:** This is a feature of Twitter that allows you to mark a tweet as one you like. To like a tweet, click the heart. Once you click it, the heart will turn red, and Twitter will automatically pin the

message to your account for reference later. When others designate your tweets as likes, you'll be notified on your Notifications
Tab. The number next to the heart indicates that within an hour
of sending this tweet, five people liked it.

Writer's Digest @WritersDigest · 1h
Write the best opening line for this prompt, & your work will be
published in @WritersDigest:ow.ly/V1Qy5

- **Follow:** Facebook has friends and fans, LinkedIn has connections, and Twitter has followers. When you decide to follow other
  users, they will receive a message (depending on their email settings) and have the option to follow you back. Even if the other
  user doesn't follow you back, you can continue to follow them
  and receive their tweets.

- **Follower:** This term is used for authors, readers, and others who
  choose to receive your tweets.

- **Handle:** A Twitter handle is the username you select. For example, @CaballoFrances.

- **# (Hashtag):** The hashtag, # (once called the pound sign), immediately precedes (without a space) one or more words. Together,
  the word(s) and symbol become a hyperlinked keyword and are
  searchable on Twitter. When using a hashtag in the Twitter search
  bar (located to the left of your profile image in the taskbar), users
  can find the type of information they are looking for. A secondary and just as important function of hashtags is that when they
  are used in a tweet, they can direct readers to your books. How?
  Let's say you write a tweet with the hashtag #HistoricalFiction and
  #novel. Readers may use one of those hashtags in the search bar to
  find a new book and, as can happen on Twitter, will discover your
  books. When you write a tweet with a hashtag, your tweet becomes
  searchable and, therefore, more discoverable. Do not include spaces
  in multi-word hashtags such as #1LineWednesday or #LoveBooks.

- Lists: You can use the Lists feature to keep track of your readers and colleagues, agents, publishers, book bloggers, or cover designers. Lists have the potential to economize your time on Twitter by allowing you to focus on the users you most want to keep track of. Here's how you can set up a list.

Navigate to your profile image to the left of the quill pen in the upper taskbar, and click on your image.

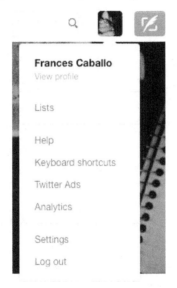

Beneath "View Profile," you will see an option to create a list and name it.

Create a list

A list is a curated group of
Twitter users and a great way
to organize your interests.
Learn more

Create new list

To add a user to your new list, navigate to that user's profile and click on the gearshift next to the follow/following button.

Click "add or remove from lists," and then place a checkmark next to your designated list.

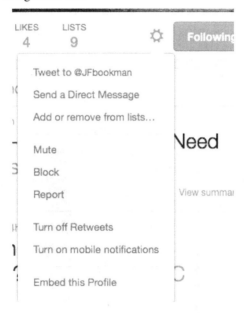

Use your lists to discover relevant information for your own retweets.

- **Mention/Retweet:** A mention occurs when someone includes your username/handle in a tweet. A retweet occurs when someone shares your tweets, or when you share a reader's tweets. RT is an abbreviation for retweet. To send a retweet while you're on Twitter, click the retweet button, as seen below. (The green icon with the number 2 next to it.) The number next to the retweet icon indicates the number of times the message has been retweeted.)

- **Modified Tweet/MT:** Some users will write MT when they send a retweet and alter the wording. MT is pointless because you can structure your tweets, including retweets, however you'd like.

- **Muting:** If you don't want to block someone, but you still don't want to see his or her tweets, you have the option to mute the user. Follow the same steps that you would use to add someone to a list or block the user. For a more in-depth explanation, refer to the section below on blocking.

- **Pinned Tweets:** You can pin a Tweet to the top of your profile page. Do this when you have a promotion you're running or when you wrote an especially good blog post you want others to read.

- **Spam:** Behaviors and actions that violate Twitter rules are considered spam. Generally, they can be any actions or tweets that others don't care for and that can risk ruining your author brand.

- **Timeline:** This word is synonymous with Home and newsfeed. Your Home Tab or Timeline is where you'll see tweets from your followers.

- **Tweeps:** This term is used to describe friends or followers with whom you are in frequent contact.

- **Tweet:** A message a user sends to his or her following that abides by the 140-character rule. It can comprise a blog title with a link, an uplifting quote, an image or video, or a question to another user. Tweets can also be expressions of gratitude or messages congratulating another user on a great blog post or new book. How often you decide to tweet depends on your availability. It's recommended that you tweet a minimum of three to five times daily.

- **Twitterati:** Similar to glitterati, the Twitterati are the stars of Twitter.

- **Twitter chat:** A Twitter chat is an active discussion occurring on Twitter at a specific time and typically for the duration of an hour. As long as you know the hashtag and time of the Twitter chat, you can join it. Twitter chats provide opportunities to connect with other writers, and book marketing and publishing experts around a specific topic and expand your network by chatting with users who are new to you. You can learn about upcoming Twitter chats by tweets your followers send a few days before the chat occurs or by using the application Twubs.com.

- **Twitterer/Tweeter:** Someone who uses Twitter.

- **Twittosphere:** Similar to Twitterverse, this term refers to a collective group of people who tweet.

- **Unfollow:** You have the option to no longer follow other users. When you unfollow someone, you'll no longer see their tweets in your newsfeed. However, if you created a list and included that user on your list, you will continue to see that person's tweets until you remove him or her from the list.

- **Via:** You can use this term when you retweet someone else's tweet or content. Here is an example: "*This Week in the Blogs, July 12–18, 2014 http://dlvr.it/6N1Gld via @JFbookman.*" RT is rarely used to signify a retweet.

- You can find an even more complete list of terms by navigating to Twitter's glossary at https://support.twitter.com/166337.

Let's Talk About Blocking Users

Is someone bugging you on Twitter? Navigate to the gearshift next to the follow button and select Block.

Tweet to @JFbookman

Send a Direct Message

Add or remove from lists...

Mute

Block

Report

Turn off Retweets

Turn on mobile notifications

Embed this Profile

Note: As you can see, you can accomplish several tasks here. You can also Mute a user. After you mute someone, you will no longer see that person's tweets but you will continue to follow him or her.

You'll have to click block a second time when the default popup appears. Twitter wants to be certain that you understand you'll no longer see this user's messages.

A Further Explanation of
Tweets, Replies, and Mentions

Where do replies appear on Twitter? The answer to that question can frustrate users. Here's the scoop:

- Twitter writes in its Help section, "Any Tweet that is a reply to you begins with your @username and will show up in the recipient's Notifications and mentions tab" and the sender's profile page.

- Twitter also says, "When a Tweet starts with a @username, the only users who will see it in their timeline (other than the sender and the recipient) are those who follow both the sender and the recipient." Translation: The Timeline (Home Tab) is a user's newsfeed.

Are you confused yet? No? Keep reading because now we're going to talk about Mentions.

A mention is a Tweet that contains another user's @username anywhere in the Tweet. Twitter says, "We collect these messages, as well as all your replies, in your Notifications tab." However, if you include multiple @usernames in a tweet, such as when you want to thank a variety of people for their retweets, Twitter will place those mentions in your followers' Notifications Tab, provided they were mentioned in the tweet.

Here are two further clarifications from Twitter:

- Replies from people with protected Tweets will be visible only to their approved followers.

- If someone sends you a reply and you are not following that user, the reply will not appear in your Home Tab. Instead, the reply will appear in your Notifications tab.

Note: When you need help, click your image in the top taskbar to the left of the quill pen and click on Help.

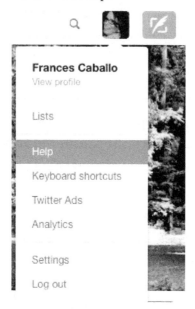

Don't Forget to Use Hashtags

As mentioned above, hashtags are composed of keywords with a pound sign directly in front of them, making hashtags hyperlinked and searchable on Twitter. Writers include hashtags to enhance search results and to highlight keywords important to their book, niche, or blog posts.

Research indicates that using more than two hashtags can reduce the number of retweets you'll receive, so use them wisely. As a practice, insert hashtags following the link in your tweet. Here's an example:

Do authors need a Facebook page? dld.bz/eJwTN #IndieAuthors

You can create distinctive hashtags to track mentions of your books. I offer a word of caution. You'll want to research your hashtag before using it to ascertain that it isn't already in use by someone else, and to check whether it might be an abbreviation for a salacious term.

To learn the definitions of hashtags or to discover what's trending on Twitter, go to tagdef.com.

Here is a list of hashtags that writers commonly use:

Note: When stringing one or more words together in a hashtag, you can capitalize the first letter of each word. There's no established practice for punctuation of multi-word hashtags but with proper capitalization, your hashtag will be easier to decipher.

#1K1H: This hashtag communicates that you're about to write 1,000 words in one hour.

#1LineWednesday, #1LineFriday: Share the best line from one of your books on Wednesdays or Fridays and use one of these hashtags.

#99c: If you have a spare $0.99 to spend on a new story, use this hashtag in your Twitter search bar and you'll find a cheap eBook. You can also use this hashtag to find new readers if you're selling an eBook for this price.

#AmazonCart: You can encourage your readers to connect their Amazon and Twitter accounts. Then each time your readers include #AmazonCart in a tweet, Amazon will know to add the items with the corresponding Amazon link to your readers' shopping carts.

#amwriting / #amediting: These terms are commonly used for Twitter chats you join. Johanna Harness is the creator of the term #amwriting as well as the www.amwriting.org website. Chats take place throughout the day. Some authors use #amediting to let their readers know that they are editing their next book.

#AuthorChat: This hashtag is used for ongoing conversations between authors.

#askagent / #askauthor: These are great hashtags for writers who don't have an agent or editor, but have questions for them. Who knows? You just might find your next editor or agent on Twitter.

#askeditor: Similar to the above hashtag, use this one to ask an editing question.

#bestseller: Have you written a best seller? Let everyone know. Refrain from using this hashtag if you haven't written a best seller. Are you reading a best seller? Show your readers that you read as well by including the title, a link, and this hashtag in a tweet.

#bibliophile / #bookworm / #reader: If you're looking for a reader for your books, add one of these hashtags to a tweet about one of your books.

#bookmarket / #bookmarketing / #GetPublished: Search for this hashtag to learn more about marketing and publishing your books.

#eBook: Did you release an ebook or recently convert a paperback novel to an ebook? Use this hashtag so that iPad, Nook, Kobo, and Kindle users can download it.

#FollowFriday / #FF: This is a fun Twitter tradition for expressing gratitude to your retweeters from the past week by giving them exposure to a wider audience. On Friday mornings, write a message composed of the user names of your most loyal retweeters. You can also use #FF to connect with writers you admire or members of your critique group or book club.

#Free / #Giveaway: This has become a popular hashtag on Twitter. Let readers know when you're offering your next book or story giveaway.

#FreebieFriday: If you offer a book giveaway on a Friday, use this hashtag.

#FridayRead: On Fridays, you can share what you're reading. Refrain from using this hashtag for your own book. Authors use this hashtag to communicate their love of reading.

#Genre / #Romantic / #Comedy / #Suspense /#Mystery / #Erotica / #DarkThriller / #DarkFantasy, etc.: Some readers search specifically by genre when looking for a new book. Use the hashtag that corresponds to your genre.

#Greatreads: You can use this hashtag for promoting your friends' books or just sharing your impressions of the last book you read.

#Holidays: #Halloween, #Christmas, #Hanukkah, and other holidays are sometimes trending on Twitter. Use them in creative ways to promote your blog and books when you feature an event or blog post related to a holiday.

#HotTitles: Have you read some books lately that are selling like wildfire? Let your Tweeps know about them. (Don't use this hashtag for your own books.)

#Instapoet: Use this hashtag to attract traffic to your Instagram account, to identify yourself as a poet who has risen through the ranks as an avid social media user, or to attract attention to similar poets.

#KidLit/#PictureBook: Authors of children's books will want to use these hashtags.

#kindle: If you have a book on Kindle, let your readers know about it.

#memoir: Connect with other memoirists and readers by using this hashtag. Also, designate your latest memoir with this hashtag.

#nanowrimo: Every November, thousands of writers take part in NaNoWriMo (National Novel Writing Month), the effort to write a novel in one month. The project started in 1989 in the San Francisco Bay Area. Over time, it became a national and then international effort. By 2013, NaNoWriMo attracted 310,000 adult novelists, plus an additional 89,500 young writers. You can keep in touch with other NaNoWriMo writers all over the world by using the #nanowrimo hashtag in your tweets or by searching for this term. Use it to let your readers know that you're writing another volume in a series you write too.

#ShortStory: Do you prefer to write short stories? Attract new admirers with this hashtag.

#ThankfulThursday: Similar to #FF, use this hashtag to thank users in your community.

#WhatToRead: Looking for a new book to read? Use this hashtag in Twitter's search bar.

#WLCAuthor: The World Literary Café is a promotional website for authors. Similar to the Independent Author Network (#IAN), Indie authors who join these organizations help each other in their promotions. NOTE: These types of hashtags are unfamiliar to your readers so use them thoughtfully, if at all.

#wordcount: With this hashtag you can share your progress with other writers on the book or story you're writing.

#writegoal: Users include this hashtag to announce publicly how many words they intend to write that day.

#WriterWednesday / #WW: Use this hashtag to connect with writers you admire and authors who are your colleagues.

#WritersBlock / #WriteMotivation: Do you sometimes need a little motivation in the mornings to get your writing started? Use these hashtags to find your inspiration. If you're also an editor, use these hashtags to inspire authors.

#WritersLife: If you have a fun image or quote to share about writing or the writing process, use this hashtag to amuse your author colleagues.

#writetip / #writingtip: If you don't have time to take a workshop, trying using these hashtags to learn more about your craft. Authors who are book coaches or editors can use these hashtags to attract new clients.

#writing / #editing: These terms are similar to #amwriting and #amediting.

#writingblitz: Use this term to let your followers know that today you are writing as fast as you can.

#writingfiction: Fiction writers use this hashtag to meet each other or to share their books, goals, or ideas on writing fiction.

#writingprompt / #writeprompt: Is it hard to get started on the next chapter of your novel? Well, worry no more. Log on to Twitter, search for this tag, and you'll find a great prompt to get those creative juices bubbling.

Popular Hashtags

#amwriting

#amreading

#IndieAuthor

#FridayReads

#quote

#quotes

#motivation

#caturday

Watch Trends to Possibly Attract New Followers

Do you ever pay attention to Trends on Twitter? You'll find trending hashtags in a white box in the left column of your Home Tab, Profile, Notifications Tab, and Moments Tab.

Trends · Change

Chelsea
606K Tweets

#CantTalkRightNowIm
12.1K Tweets

Star Trek
88.8K Tweets

#The100
61.9K Tweets

#BackInTimeForChristmas
Trending for 2 hours now

Trends are hashtags that are being used thousands of times or even millions of times during the day.

You can determine the type of trending issues you'd like to be notified of by clicking Change and deciding whether you prefer notifications of trends by geographic region or tailored by the type of tweets you send. If you select the tailored option, Twitter will also include news-related trending hashtags.

Some trends are fun, some are news items, and some are there because marketing companies created them.

Once I noticed that #UKYAchat was trending. #UKYA stands for Young Adult Books written by United-Kingdom-based authors. If you are a YA writer, you'll want to watch for that one appearing again.

Another day, #picturebooks was trending. Do you write picture books? Watch for this one. Two years ago, #IReadEverywhere was created and promoted by a library in New York. That hashtag caught on fire.

Sometimes trending hashtags are silly, such as #ICantStopSmilingBecause.

My point is that you need to check the Trends box daily. Yes, some of them will be on topics unrelated to writing or any of your interests, but some of them will apply to you or one of your books. Almost daily, there's one writing-related trending hashtag.

Include a hashtag with your tweets, and don't forget to check trending hashtags every morning. You just might be amazed at how using fashionable hashtags of the moment will bring new followers—and maybe even new readers—into your sphere.

Chapter 7
Guidelines for
the Advanced Twitter User

*Twitter is fun because it lets me stay in touch with
all my original readers who grew up with my books.*
R.L. Stein

Have you been using Twitter for a year or longer? Then you may benefit from the suggestions in this book.

First, let's take a look at Twitter's social demographics. The information below is from the Pew Research Center's Internet, Science & Tech Division, which published "The Demographics of Social Media Users."

- 37% of online users between 18 and 29 use Twitter.

- 54% of users have attended college.

Does this mean that if your readers are 45+ years of age that you should ignore Twitter? No. Most of my blog and website visitors are 45+ years of age and yet Twitter is the #1 source of referral traffic to my website.

The above numbers provide a general rule. Users of all ages use Twitter, as do many readers, literary agents, editors, book reviewers and bloggers, and publishing experts, but the younger ages dominate. You need to pay attention to your website's analytics from Google (your webmaster can help you with this) and determine if Twitter is hitting your target readership. Then determine whether Twitter is a valuable tool for you in terms of meeting experts who can help you with your career as an author.

Tweet Images to Boost Engagement

Social media has increasingly become a visual platform, and that's as true for Twitter as it is for Pinterest, Instagram, Tumblr, and YouTube. Images pique interest and attract the eye more than blocks of black text.

When I started focusing on tweeting one image daily, engagement soared on my account. Retweets went up by 24.4%, and likes went up by 43.1%.

Engagement
Engagement on Twitter is defined as interactions anywhere in the tweet, including clicks on your avatar as well as the number of retweets, replies, follows, and likes your tweets generate.

Impressions
Impressions represent the number of times someone sees your tweet/ image.

Below is an image that garnered nearly 5,000 impressions, 12 replies, 51 retweets, and 68 likes.

Top Tweet earned 4,928 impressions

Do you get your best ideas for your stories during the night? #amwriting
pic.twitter.com/S1w9GnRofX

IN THE MIDDLE OF THE NIGHT,..

↰ 12   ⇄ 51   ♥ 68

If you want to increase engagement on Twitter, take the time to use images with all of your tweets, if possible. And make sure that the images resonate with your readers and followers.

Tweeting Controversial Issues That Are Trending

What if the topic that's trending is controversial? Should you wade into those waters?

Let me give you an example. In my community in Northern California, there was an officer-involved killing of a youth, Andy Lopez, who was walking near his home one afternoon while holding an Airsoft shotgun—a toy—that resembled an AK-47 assault rifle. An officer shot and killed the teenager.

As I reeled from the incident that occurred one mile from my home, the killing of Michael Brown and protests in Ferguson captured the nation's attention.

Could I tweet about the Ferguson incident even though it didn't strictly relate to my audience? I decided to take a chance.

I retweeted information posted by Antonio French. French is an alderman and founder of a community education nonprofit called North Campus. French, who had 1,026 followers as of August 15, 2014, was one of the protesters arrested and then quickly released.

He caught MSNBC's attention and now has a verified account with 128,000 followers and follows just 1,679 people.

My intent when I retweeted Antonio French was not to grow my following or expand my influence, but to express sorrow and join the community of Twitter users who were also concerned about what happened to Michael Brown and the protests that ensued in the shooting's aftermath.

With social media, it's important to remain true to yourself. Using Twitter or any other social media network for the sole purpose of marketing your book is never advisable. The social nature of these platforms requires users to share more than just a link to Amazon or iTunes.

I want to make three points here:

1. When you strike a chord with your audience—in your case, readers—they will follow you en masse.

2. Select your topics carefully. I would not tweet about abortion or religion because those subjects are too divisive.

3. It's okay to occasionally tweet about issues unrelated to your book or readers. The point isn't to jump on hot, social issues in hopes of finding new readers. The greater goal is the importance of being a thoughtful citizen of your community, nation, and the world, and to share your compassion for others.

I'm not suggesting that writers chase controversy. However, if you wrote a historical novel that was set during the civil rights struggle, you might have wanted to join conversations like the one that occurred on Twitter. Or, if you wrote a nonfiction book about racial struggles around the world, this might have been the type of conversation you would have wanted to join.

Tweeting Memes and Sharing Expressions of Sorrow

I've always been a huge fan of Robin Williams. The day after his death, I tweeted quotes by him, and those messages attracted numerous retweets. His death was tragic, and I wanted to join the virtual community of fans who also felt a profound sense of loss.

Also, Williams lived in the North Bay Area where I live. He owned a home in my county and supported local nonprofits, so to join the conversation made sense for me. He was also an artist and someone who was incredibly talented and creative.

Trending issues can also be memes and phrases. During the 2014 World Cup, #BecauseofFútbol was a trending phrase. Using this hashtag, a writer could have sent this message: "#BecauseofFútbol I didn't finish my short story today." Or, "#BecauseofFútbol I missed my editor's deadline."

Another trending issue at one time was #sometimesyouhaveto. A writer might tweet: "#sometimesyouhaveto turn off the Wi-Fi to get your writing done." Or you might tweet: "#sometimesyouhaveto kill a character to make the novel work."

#FridayReads is a popular hashtag. Use the opportunity to promote the books of other authors and perhaps they'll return the favor.

You can also use the holidays to your advantage. You might send this tweet: "The perfect #Christmas gift for your #bibliophile is (then add the name of your book and a link to where it can be purchased)." Or you could say, "What's scarier than a goblin on #Halloween? My new thriller."

I encourage you to also use holidays to promote your colleagues' books and books by authors you admire.

Be creative with how you market your books. Join discussions and Twitter chats, monitor trends, tweet hashtags that offer new avenues to reach potential readers, and share your grief with a virtual community of mourners.

Above all, focus on what works on social media: being authentic as an author and as a human being who cares about what happens in your community, however you define it.

How to Understand Twitter's Analytics

There are applications that can measure tweets, followers, and other benchmarks, but it's unnecessary to pay for these analytics when Twitter provides them for free.

Once you've logged into your Twitter account, type analytics.twitter. com. You can see your top tweets and access your analytics when you click on the graph that appears on your Profile page, just beneath a collection of your images and to the left of your tweets.

When you click on the graph to access your analytics, instead of arriving at your dashboard you will access your top-performing tweets.

Definitions of Twitter Terms

The most difficult aspect to understanding your analytics is deciphering the terms Twitter uses. Below, are some of the more common terms.

- Detail expands: Click a Tweet to view more details—This means that once you click on the View Tweet Activity icon, which is a tiny bar graph, analytics for that tweet will open as in the example here:

- Embedded media Clicks: Clicks to view a photo or video in the Tweet—This measures the number of times another user clicks on a video to play it.

- Engagements: The total number of times users interact with a Tweet, including retweets, replies, follows, and likes

- Likes: The number of times a user liked a Tweet

- Follows: The number of times a user followed you directly from the Tweet

- Hashtag Clicks: Clicks on hashtag(s) in the Tweet

- Impressions: The number of times another user sees your tweet either in his or her Timeline or as a result of a search

- Replies: Times a user replied to a Tweet

- Retweets: Number of times users retweeted a Tweet

- Shared via email: Times a user emailed a Tweet to someone

- User profile Clicks: Clicks on the name, @handle, or profile photo of the person who authors a tweet

How to Use Twitter Analytics

Reviewing your Twitter analytics will tell you a great deal about your followers, including your readers.

When you first open your analytics, you will see an overview of your account covering the past 28 days with information on how the data has changed.

To the right you'll see data for the current month for tweets, profile visits, new followers you've acquired, tweet impressions, mentions, and tweets linking to your account.

The bulk of the data in the overview will list highlights for the tweets you've sent.

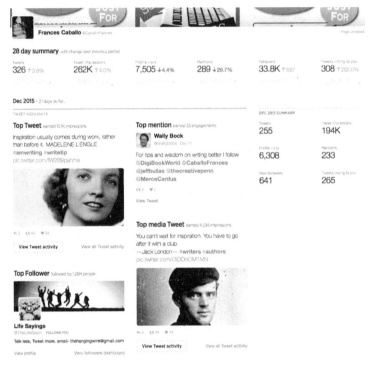

There are five tabs with additional statistics. You'll find them in the taskbar of your Twitter analytics page. Here they are:

- Tweets
- Audiences
- Twitter Cards
- Events

More

Under More, you can find analytics for Twitter ads you set up.

The tab on tweets demonstrates the number of impressions your tweets made over the previous 28 days. Impressions are the number of times users saw your tweets.

Twitter provides a graphic overview and then drills down, showing each tweet's performance regarding Impressions, Engagements, and Engagement Rate. There's also graphic information on the right column of the page.

When I click twice on the top tweet, a quote by Madeleine L'Engle, I can glean more analytic data about the tweet.

Impressions	10,221
Total engagements	224
Media engagements	91
Likes	54
Retweets	43
Detail expands	16
Link clicks	8
Profile clicks	8
Replies	3
Hashtag clicks	1

In the right column of the Tweets tab you'll find these graphs:

Audiences

The next tab provides fascinating demographic information about followers who interact with you.

Under the Audiences tab, you'll see an Overview, and data for Demographics, Lifestyle, Consumer Behavior, and Mobile Footprint.

You can learn about your audience's interests, occupations, gender, net worth, marital status, education attained, and whether they rent or own their home.

Demographics

Under this section, you can learn additional details about your audience's occupations, country of origin, net worth, and household income.

Lifestyle

Under this tab, you can discover your followers' political party affiliations, the TV genres they prefer, and their interests.

The Consumer Behavior and Mobile Footprint Information is better suited for big brands, such as Mercedes or Honda.

Why is all this data important? Clearly, much of it helps Apple, Mercedes, and other big brands determine how to structure their advertising. And you can use some of this data to learn about your readers, especially their gender and country of origin.

Twitter Cards

This is the next main tab. Working with your webmaster, you can enable Twitter Cards for your website. Once they're enabled, every time someone sends a tweet from your website, an image will be included. The cards can include photos and videos.

There are three sub-tabs here: URL Clicks, Install Attempts, and Retweets

URL Clicks equal the numbers of Clicks on a URL in a tweet or a card. This is how the data appears for URL Clicks:

Snapshot
A quick glance at how Tweets with your Twitter Cards drove URL clicks.

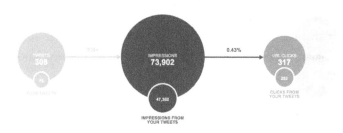

Change over time
How Tweets with your Twitter Cards affected your impressions and clicks from **Nov 24 – Dec 21, 2015**

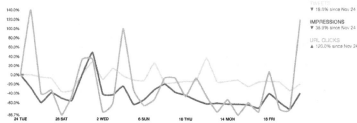

Install Attempts
This data represents the number of times a user Clicks an application "call to action" (Get the App) from within a Twitter card to enable the app.

Retweets
The retweets tallied here are for tweets containing a link to your content. Here is a snapshot glance.

Why should you bother with your analytics? They will inform you about your followers and provide valuable information about the performance of your tweets.

Growing your following is fine, but what's even more important is engaging with your following. The analytics that Twitter provides informs you about the performance of your tweets; whether your following is engaging with you; and whether you need to change your tweets, add more images, or continue your present course.

The more information you can glean, the better you can market your books and engage with your readers.

Who to Follow on Twitter

Here are some of the people I follow and keep track of on Twitter. You'll enjoy their tweets, blog posts, and ideas on blogging, writing, and book marketing.

Joel Friedlander—@JFbookman
Jane Friedman—@JaneFriedman
Joanna Penn—@thecreativepenn
LisaTener—@LisaTener
Penny Sansevieri—@Bookgal
BookWorks—@BookWorksNYC
Orna Ross—@OrnaRoss
Elizabeth S. Craig—@elizabethscraig
Porter Anderson—@Porter_Anderson
Writer Unboxed—@WriterUnboxed
Anne R. Allen—@annerallen
Betty Sargent—@BookWorksBetty
K.M. Weiland—@KMWeiland
Dan Blank—@DanBlank

Chapter 8
Tweets and Actions to Avoid on Twitter

If you haven't been using Twitter for long, you may not know that there are certain etiquette rules on this microblogging network. And if you don't follow them, you may have trouble growing your tribe. I've consolidated the verboten activities below.

4 Tweets to Never Send

If you've reviewed the initial documents, you know by now what you should do and what tweets are good to send. Here is a list of tweets your followers won't appreciate.

1. Stop sending tweets announcing how many people you followed or unfollowed using one of many applications, such as Tweepi or JustUnfollow. These types of tweets promote companies while diluting your brand messaging.

2. Don't send direct messages to your new followers asking them to check out your website, blog, stories, books, or poetry. In fact, stop sending direct messages unless you're trying to contact someone you know to convey your email address or phone number.

3. Think twice before sending someone a thank you for following. In the early days, these tweets were common, but we've matured

since then. Your time can be better spent doing something more worthwhile, such as writing a blog post, working on your next book, or finding great content to retweet.

4. Don't send five or seven or ten tweets in a row. It's not a good practice to flood someone's timeline with a day's worth of messages in the span of a few minutes.

Actions to Reconsider

Even if you're a fairly seasoned Twitter user, it might be a good idea to review some of these faux pas. Why? They may be preventing you from attracting more readers, book reviewers, and book bloggers from following you.

Here they are:

1. This rule bears repeating: Did you upload an image of your cat, dog, book cover, or favorite lake as your avatar? Or, are you an egghead, using the default egg as your avatar? Your avatar needs to be a professionally taken picture of you, the author. If you don't want to hire a photographer, ask a friend to take a picture of you, and don't smirk or make a funny face in it.

2. Create a header image; don't leave it blank. You can use a variety of free applications, such as Canva or PicMonkey. You can add your book covers, announce the publication of a new book, or use an image that reflects a scene in your book. You can download a free image from Unsplash or Pixabay, or use a picture you took.

3. Refrain from writing a senseless bio, littered with hashtags, such as #cappuccino #frappuccino #kittens #puppies #writer #reader #blogger #rescueddogs. Write a professional bio instead. Your Twitter avatar and bio are searchable on the Internet, and you want to use your Twitter profile to advance your author brand and your professional appearance.

4. Don't use all 140 characters available to you when you tweet. Instead, keep your tweets to between 110 and 120 characters. Using fewer than 140 characters will give others a chance to retweet you without having to reconfigure your message. And there will be room for your username to credit you as the author of the content.

5. Are you #doing #this #with #your #hashtags in your #tweets? Refrain from using more than two hashtags because the more hashtags you use, the fewer retweets you'll receive.

6. Are you interacting with other authors? If you're not, you're missing a huge opportunity to collaborate and co-market books and blogs. It's important to be friendly on Twitter, meet other authors—including those who write in your genre (perhaps especially those authors)—and promote other authors. The more authors you meet and promote, the more they will suggest your books to their readers.

7. Never retweet tweets that praise you or your book. Retweeting tweets of praise is like laughing at your own jokes—when the jokes aren't even funny. Promoting yourself in this manner is akin to bragging.

8. Are you ignoring the 80/20 rule? Guess what? Social media, including Twitter, isn't about you. It's not even about your book, poetry, blog, or website. Social media is about engagement first and content second. Make sure that 80 percent of your content comes from a variety of sources and that you restrict your own content to only 20 percent of your tweets.

9. Are you responding to replies or questions? If not, you're missing an opportunity to engage with your readers and colleagues. Engaging with other users is the single most important aspect of social media. Don't neglect this important activity.

10. Never sign up for an application that sends automatic direct messages thanking people for following and directing new followers to your blog or book. These messages are the scourge of Twitter.

11. Are you tweeting only between 9 a.m. and 5 p.m.? No one expects your account to be a 24/7 operation, but your followers don't log off when you start preparing dinner. You're tweeting to a world-wide audience, so schedule some tweets early and some late.

12. How often are you tweeting? Tweeting too often can be problematic for your followers. There's no set formula for how often you should be tweeting. However, unless you're the most interesting person in the world, chances are if you're clogging up their timelines, they'll get turned off in a hurry. Space your tweets at least two hours apart.

13. Use caution when punctuating your tweets with exclamation points or using ALL CAPS. You wouldn't yell at your readers in person, so don't do it on Twitter. Use exclamation points sparingly and when in doubt, one is enough. Or skip them entirely.

14. Don't use the application TrueTwit.com. This application promises to prevent spammers from following you, but what it will do is hamper your ability to grow a following. If you want to get rid of spammers, review your followers list every day and block spammers; or use ManageFlitter, which identifies unfollowers as well as inactive, spam, and bot accounts. Avoid TrueTwit at all cost.

Chapter 9
LinkedIn:
The Nonfiction Authors' Haven

Fiction is like a spider's web, attached ever so slightly perhaps,
but still attached to life at all four corners.
Often the attachment is scarcely perceptible.
Virginia Woolf

Everyone gravitates to Facebook because, for the most part, it's warm and fuzzy. Your friends are on it, family members use it, and your book club or writing group might even have an active Facebook group. People share heartwarming stories, funny anecdotes, and pictures they take. Reading through your Facebook News Feed can bring you to laughter or tears or, in some cases, anger. Like the books of Nicholas Sparks, Facebook is a breezy read.

LinkedIn, on the other hand, is a brawny social media network for professionals. As some social media pundits note, LinkedIn is Facebook with a tie. Well, not exactly. It's a platform that requires precision, thought, and detail. In some ways, it's the Virginia Woolf of social media. In Woolf 's novels, you won't find any unnecessary detail. From the opening words of *Mrs. Dalloway* to the book's concluding sentence, every event of the day and every thought carry significance.

Setting up a LinkedIn account can appear easy. It isn't. There is care and planning involved in setting up your profile, listing your experience, and shining a light on your skills and accomplishments. This shouldn't dissuade you from using LinkedIn because it's an important social media network, especially for nonfiction writers. Fiction authors can benefit mostly from the groups, where you can share your expertise and learn from colleagues.

Unlike Facebook, on LinkedIn you can post your finest, keyword-rich resume of experience, find freelance writing gigs, and search for editors, publishers, agents, illustrators, graphic designers, and marketing professionals. With more than 450 million users, LinkedIn can be an integral component of your social media marketing plan, provided you write nonfiction.

When I wrote the first edition of this book, I felt that LinkedIn was as important to fiction authors as to nonfiction writers. I no longer believe that to be true. What would a romance writer do on LinkedIn? Learn about marketing, I suppose. It's better to create your profiles and engage with romance book readers on Facebook. The only reason to have a profile on LinkedIn is if you want to join groups to learn more about book production and promotion.

LinkedIn can be a nice break from some of the chatter on Facebook. On LinkedIn, you won't find pictures of brides or news about a dog's weight-loss program. Cutesy kitten pictures, declarations of love, and photos of gluten-free lasagna don't belong on this venue. Instead, you'll connect with other writers interested in publishing and promoting their books. Learn from them, share information, and do what LinkedIn is designed to accomplish: help you to connect professionally with other users who share your passion for writing, want to improve their craft, and want to see their books get out into the world and sell.

Break out of your introverted shell and participate in groups, discover books you want to purchase, meet bloggers you admire, and encounter some talented people who have expert advice to share.

How to Get Started on LinkedIn

LinkedIn launched in 2002 and began taking sign-ups in 2003. By 2008 it was a global company, opening its first international office in London and starting French and Spanish versions of its platform.

According to the Pew Research Center, these statistics describe its current user base.

- LinkedIn attracts an educated audience that tends to be urban and has a good income.

- The age groups trend toward the 18–29 years of age crowd, and 30–49 year olds.

- Sixty-one percent of its users are either urban or suburban.

- Seventy-five percent of its users earn more than $50,000 per year.

- The majority of users are college graduates or have some college experience.

Start by Creating a Profile

To start using LinkedIn, navigate to www.linkedin.com and sign up. LinkedIn allows 20 characters for your first name and 40 for your last name. Upload a photo of yourself that conveys a professional image. Don't use the cover of one of your books or a picture of your dog or cat.

The dimensions of your profile picture need to be a minimum of 200 × 200 pixels and a maximum of 500 × 500.

Next, add a background image to the top of your profile. The correct photo dimensions are between 1000 × 425 and 4000 × 4000. The background image will be long and narrow. The image needs to be:

- File type .JPG, .GIF, or .PNG

- No larger than 4MB

If you have a LinkedIn business page—and some experts will encourage you to do this— then the standard logo should be 100 pixels wide by 60 pixels high. If you have a square logo, then the dimensions are 50 × 50. Images appear best in news feeds when you size them at 800 × 400.

Do you need a company page? Most Indie authors don't. If you have a business that's related to your nonfiction writing, then you'll want to consider this option. You'll need to have a business page if you're interested in purchasing advertising.

LinkedIn's Dashboard Is a Snapshot of You

Spend time on the top dashboard. This portion of your profile needs to contain the information you want others to know about you and your book—immediately. Use keywords here: words that a potential reader or author who is looking for an editor or book coach would type when using a search engine such as Google to find you.

The Headline

The first line that appears in large text next to your photo is your name. Beneath your name is the headline. In this space, establish the reason you are on LinkedIn, and use keywords in your description. Select your words judiciously because LinkedIn limits you to 120 characters.

A nonfiction book coach on LinkedIn uses this as her headline:

Brand Business With a Book | eBook Writing | Self-Publishing | Book Marketing | 25-Year Writing Coach
It's succinct, and the capitalization draws attention to the primary foci of her business. She repeats this information further down, too, next to the word Current. This is an example of astute marketing on LinkedIn. If you are uncertain about how to present yourself, peruse LinkedIn and read other users' profiles, especially those of other writers, editors, and creative writing instructors. Decide what your salient trait is and how it distinguishes you from other writers in the world. Then write your headline and draw attention to whatever it is that makes you unique in your field.

Do you write fiction? Don't call yourself a publisher or say you own a publishing company and then provide the name of it. Instead, write a headline similar to this suggestion:

Author of (plug in your genre) novel (and add the name of our most recent book or two)
For example, your headline could be similar to this example:

Author of She Stole My Soul Mate and Revenge
This is what my headline says:

Social Media Manager & Strategist for Writers | Author's Guide to Goodreads | Social Media in 30 Minutes a Day

I listed my career and the titles of my two most recently published books.

If you are uncertain about how to present yourself, peruse LinkedIn and read other users' profiles, especially those of other writers, editors, and book coaches. Decide what your salient trait is and how it distinguishes you from other writers in the world. Then write your headline and draw attention to whatever it is that makes you unique in your field.

When you determine what your most important keywords are, repeat them. Use them in your headline and below in the summary. List your specialties as well, and any courses you've developed. LinkedIn gives you ample space to insert your keywords throughout your profile.

Contact Information

When visitors click on your contact information in the lower, right-hand corner of the dashboard, a window opens listing your website, blog, and designated landing pages. Instead of settling for LinkedIn's default language such as "company website" or "blog," use your blog title or the name of your book, and include links to your blog, Amazon, Kobo, and the iBooks Store on iTunes, or wherever people can purchase your book.

In my example, I've listed a link to my website, the landing page that lists all of my books, and the landing page where writers can subscribe to my free email course.

To customize your links, follow these steps:

- On the top toolbar, hover over Profile, and then click Edit Profile.

- Click Contact Info.

- Click Other and type the title of your page.

Claiming a Vanity URL Isn't Vain

You don't need to settle for a URL with a series of numbers in it. You can instead create your vanity URL and use it to market yourself on other online venues. For example, my vanity URL is www.linkedin.com/francescaballo. Here are the steps you'll need to follow:

1. On the top menu bar, hover over Profile, and then click Edit Profile.

2. Click Contact Info.

3. Move your cursor over the link, and click the Settings icon next to it.

4. Customize it to your name and click Save.

Attempt to use your first and last names. LinkedIn will check to see if your vanity URL is available. If it is, you now own it. If not, you'll have to make another attempt until you get a URL that's available.

If another user has taken your name, use a close approximation of your name. For example, if you have a middle initial, use it. Or reverse the order of your first and last names.

Optimize Your Summary

Use the summary to succinctly explain to people why they would love your books, or retain you for training, editing services, or coaching. A succinct synopsis that explains who you are, what you do, and the benefits readers, writers, and other clients would gain by reading your books or attending your workshops receives excellent visibility here. Some people consider the summary as their cover letter to the world.

LinkedIn allows up to 2,000 characters, including spaces, for the summary. Few if any people would read a summary of that length.

Add to this section the titles and benefits of your books. If you wrote a cookbook, explain how the book will save readers time, teach them to cook like a professional chef, or show them how to make sensational Snickerdoodles.

If you write for the Young Adult demographic, explain why high schools should include your book in their English classes. Suppose you wrote a grammar book. Inform junior high English teachers and school administrators about the benefits of your instructional manual.

Did you write a crime or mystery book? Mention what award it received. Do you teach memoir workshops? Include the benefits of attending your sessions. As much as you can, enrich this section with keywords, and use bullets to market your book or services as best you can.

You can add links to your summary and even upload a free ebook, video, white paper, or tips sheet, as well as links to your favorite landing pages.

Skills and Endorsements

You will want to showcase your talents by adding the Skills and Endorsements section to your profile.

1. Select Edit Profile and scroll down to the Skills & Endorsements section.

2. Click the Edit icon in the upper right.

3. Type the name of the skill you wish to highlight, and then select it from the drop-down list that appears. If you don't see the skill you'd like to add, type the skill and click on Add, and then click Save.

To add skills in the future, click Edit Profile, scroll down to this section, and click the blue and white +Add Skill box.

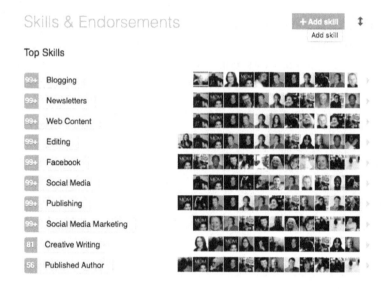

LinkedIn allows you to add up to 50 skills; appearing first will be the skills with the most endorsements. Sometimes other users will endorse you for skills you haven't selected, and you'll need to decide whether those skills apply to you or whether the expanded skills will dilute your brand rather than secure your niche. (Note: As of this writing, LinkedIn is in discussions about altering how Endorsements work. They might be deleted from user's profiles. Stay tuned.)

If you'd like to remove endorsements from your profile, follow these steps:

1. Return to Profile > Edit Profile.

2. Click the X next to the skills you'd like to remove.

3. Click Save.

Recommendations

Endorsements are different from recommendations. Above, you saw how endorsements work. Recommendations are like testimonials on your website or reviews on Amazon. They demonstrate to your contacts that people enjoy reading your books or working with you.

LinkedIn has certain parameters about how you can incorporate a recommendation into your profile. You need to request the testimonial through LinkedIn, and once it arrives, you can't alter it, not even to correct a typo.

To request a recommendation from a colleague, go to your Privacy and Settings page. Follow these directions:

Move your cursor over your photo on the taskbar of your homepage, and select Privacy & Settings > Manage.

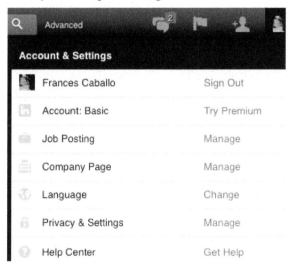

1. LinkedIn will prompt you to sign into your account.

2. Click the Manage Your Recommendations link under Privacy Controls.

3. Click the Ask for a Recommendation link at the top of the page.

4. Select a position/job category.

5. Type the name of your contact in the search bar in step No. 2.

6. Enter your request in the Create your message section. Don't use the default message; personalize it.

7. Click Send.

Once you receive recommendations, the complete text of the testimonials will appear farther down on your profile, within the experience section. Testimonials are important because they will give you credibility as a writer or expert and provide further insight into your books, writing, and editing or coaching skills.

Don't Be a Loner—Join Groups

Groups are perhaps the most important feature on LinkedIn. In some cases, they have the potential to highlight you as a thought leader in the publishing industry. In other cases, the groups can offer answers to your marketing, writing, and publishing questions.

Groups also let you meet new contacts with whom you can connect on other platforms. Sharing experiences and learning from the experiences of other writers is what makes the group feature so popular.

A word of caution: Never try to promote your books, blog posts, or your services in your groups. Instead, talk about your publishing experiences, recommend book cover designers, offer your best marketing tips, and share information you've gleaned from your self-publishing experience. To find a specific type of group, click the bars to the left of the search bar and select Groups from the drop-down menu.

Here are a few groups you can consider joining:

- Book Marketing
- Books and Writers
- Fiction Writers and Editors
- Published & Emerging Writers of Fiction & Nonfiction
- Indie Authors
- Book Writer
- New Authors

In January 2016, LinkedIn made these changes to its groups:

1. All groups are private and on a members-only basis. Group moderators will need to accept you into a group before you can participate.

2. The content you wish to add won't automatically appear on a group's page. Moderators will review all content.

3. Groups don't have subgroups.

4. RSS feeds aren't allowed. In other words, you can't add your blog posts to groups. This step was taken to avoid spam.

5. LinkedIn's algorithm filters posts that are promotional in nature.

6. You can communicate with your groups via an iOS (Apple) mobile app. Get the app from Apple's App Store.

7. If you're an Android user, get your mobile app at Google Play.

Help Search Engines Find You

Wouldn't you like every aspect of your LinkedIn profile to be visible to search engines? To make this possible, you need to go to your settings. Here are the steps.

1. Log into your account and click Privacy & Settings.

2. You will be prompted to log in again.

3. Under Profile, click Edit Your Public Profile.

4. You will navigate back to your profile.

5. Click the arrow to View Profile As.

6. Select Manage Public Profile Settings.

7. You will navigate to another page. Click all sections you'd like to be public.

8. Click Save.

Experience and Causes

Use this section to include your volunteer experience. Everyone likes to see that professionals are giving back to their communities wherever they live.

Publications

You may add information about your books, white papers, and magazine articles in a separate section where LinkedIn will hyperlink your book titles once you add the link or URL. To do this, follow these instructions:

1. Go to Profile, and then Edit Profile.

2. Did you already add this section? Great. Then just click +Add.

3. If you haven't yet added this section to your summary, scroll up to the summary at the top and add publications to your profile by clicking Add Publications.

4. Click Add publications.

5. Insert the names of your books, a link to them (preferably the landing page on your website), and some information. Then click save.

6. Repeat the process if you have additional books.

Best Practices

Here are a few tips to get you started.

1. If you're on Twitter, include your Twitter handle on your LinkedIn profile but don't link the accounts.

2. List the books you've published, stories that are included in anthologies, and workshops you've taught.

3. Adjust your settings so that you receive emails whenever someone requests a connection or sends you an Inmail, the private messaging feature on LinkedIn.

4. Join a few groups and become an active participant by sharing your views and expertise, answering questions, and asking others for help. LinkedIn users tend to be active group participants.

5. The search bar on LinkedIn has a drop-down menu that allows users to search for people, groups, or companies. Use this feature to find other writers, agents, publishers, and groups.

6. Expand your network by searching for first-degree connections (people for whom you have email addresses, or you've communicated with in a LinkedIn group). Note: Unlike Facebook, you can't connect with people you don't know.

7. Invite writers you meet to write a guest blog post for you, or interview them on your blog.

8. Twice a day, or at least once, post an update that includes a link to some great content that others will want to read. The rule is 80% of the time you promote other colleagues or experts in the field, and 20% of the time you can post an update from your blog or about one of your books.

9. LinkedIn expanded its character limit for updates from 160 to 700 words. My advice? Keep your update concise.

10. If you've written a how-to, editing, craft, or grammar book, become an expert in LinkedIn Answers. Anyone with a LinkedIn account can use this feature to post questions and then wait for an expert—like you, perhaps—to provide the answers they need.

11. If you meet someone through a LinkedIn group who helps you, offer to write a recommendation for that person.

12. When people connect with you, don't send them a private message asking them to buy your book or read your blog.

13. Don't cross-post your tweets to LinkedIn or vice versa. Each network has its own language, and it's best to write original messages for each social media channel.

LinkedIn is a valuable resource for writers, but it will take perseverance to master and finesse the finer points of this social media channel.

For many—but not all—writers, it is a must-have platform for marketing books and enriching search engine optimization strategies. For those writers who might not benefit from all of LinkedIn's features, it's at least important to create a profile.

How to Use LinkedIn's Blogging Platform

What I like most about LinkedIn these days—and this is a way to step up your author presence on LinkedIn—is LinkedIn's publishing platform. If you haven't used it, you're in for a treat.

This is how it works. Once you write a new post for your blog, let it sit on your website for a week or longer, and then add it to LinkedIn's publishing feature.

Simply log into your account, click on Home if you don't automatically navigate to your news feed, and click on *Write an Article*.

Or, go to your profile and click +*Write a new post*.

Clicking one of these links will take you to LinkedIn's publishing platform. It will look like this:

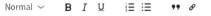

Headline

Write here. Add images or a video for visual impact.

Next, follow these steps.

1. Upload the image for your blog.

2. Add your headline.

3. Copy your recent blog post and paste it here.

4. Check the spelling.

5. Add links and highlights.

6. Add tags, also called keywords.

7. Click publish.

Next, you can tweet this post from here and write a new LinkedIn update.

Why should you take advantage of LinkedIn's publishing platform? *Publishing on LinkedIn will extend the life of your post.*

In addition to blog posts, share your videos from YouTube, Vimeo, and Vine; add information about PDFs you publish; and include tips sheets you create.

First- and Second-Degree Connections Explained

On Twitter you have followers; on Facebook you have friends and fans; and on LinkedIn your have first-degree, second-degree, and third-degree connections. Are you confused? You're not alone.

Unlike on Facebook, you can't send LinkedIn requests to connect to just anyone. LinkedIn needs to determine that you might know this person through your stated occupations, groups, or volunteer commitments. If a connection doesn't directly make sense to LinkedIn, it will ask you for that person's email address or query you as to how you know that person.

So straight from LinkedIn, here are the definitions for each type of connection.

1st-degree—People you're directly connected to because you've accepted their invitation to connect, or they've accepted your invitation.

You'll see a 1st-degree icon next to their names in search results and on their profiles. You can contact them by sending a message on LinkedIn.

2nd-degree—People who are connected to your 1st-degree connections. You'll see a 2nd-degree icon next to their names in search results and on their profiles. You can send them an invitation by clicking Connect or contacting them through an InMail. Learn more about InMail.

3rd-degree—People who are connected to your 2nd-degree connections. You'll see a 3rd-degree icon next to their names in search results and on their profiles.

- If their full first and last names are displayed, you can send them an invitation by clicking Connect.

- If only the first letter of the last name is displayed, clicking Connect isn't an option, but you can contact them through LinkedIn's private Inmail.

Fellow members of your LinkedIn groups—These people are considered part of your network because you're members of the same group. You'll see a Group icon next to their names in search results and on their profiles. You can contact them by sending a message on LinkedIn or through the group.

Resource: LinkedIn Character Limits

As you set up your LinkedIn profile or revise it, keep these character limits in mind.

LinkedIn Profile
First Name: 20 characters
Last Name: 40 characters
Headline in top panel: 120 characters
Summary: 2,000 characters
Website Anchor Text: 30 characters
Website URL: 256 maximum characters

Vanity URL: 29 characters starting after this part of the URL www.
linkedin.com/in/

Position Title: 100 characters.

Position Description: 200 minimum and 2,000 maximum

Interests: 1,000 characters

Skills: You may add up to 50 skills, with a maximum of 80 characters
per skill you create

LinkedIn Status Update: 600 characters, or 250 if including a link

Note: As with all social media, character counts include spaces.

Company Page

Company Name: 100 characters maximum

Summary: 2,000 maximum

Updates: 600 characters, or 250 if including a link

Specialties: 10 specialties, 256 maximum characters total

Website URL: 256 maximum characters

LinkedIn Publisher (Blogging Feature)

LinkedIn Publisher Post Headline: 100 maximum characters

LinkedIn Publisher Post Body Text: 40,000 characters

Chapter 10
Visual Marketing:
Images Trump Text

Content will demand more visual mediums.
Jayson DeMers

A number of years ago, experts predicted that by 2014, mobile marketing would rule the Internet. They were right.

So what's the next trend? It's already here, and it's visual marketing.

In 2015, the Pew Research Center reported that Instagram was the fourth most used social media network behind Facebook, LinkedIn, and Pinterest. That's right Pinterest, another visually-based social media network.

Why are images so hot? Mike Parkinson, the founder of Billion Dollar Graphics (BDG), explained the reason in an article titled "The Power of Visual Communication." In that report, he noted that we process visuals 60,000 times faster than text.

Images encompass various forms of imagery from blog post images to infographics to social media images. Visual communication—regardless of the medium—grabs our attention more than text.

They grab so much attention that once you incorporate more pictures into your blog and marketing, your readership and engagement will rise. Look at these statistics, cited by HubSpot, a tech company.

- Researchers found that colored visuals increased people's willingness to read a piece of content by 80%.

- Content with relevant images gets 94% more views than content without relevant images.

- Shoppers who view video are 1.81X more likely to purchase than non-viewers.

- Between April 2015 and November 2015, the amount of average daily video views on Facebook doubled from 4 billion video views per day to 8 billion.

- Syndacast predicts 74% of all Internet traffic in 2017 will be video.

- Articles with an image once every 75-100 words got double the number of social shares than articles with fewer images.

Interpreting these statistics for authors, we can conclude:

- Adding relevant images to your blog posts will increase views and adding colored visuals will increase readership by a whopping 80%.

- Want to sell more books? Consider purchasing a book trailer, and if you're a nonfiction author, create tutorial videos and upload them to your YouTube channel. Or if you have a podcast, do what many podcasters do: Record the interview as a video in addition to an audio broadcast, and upload the video to YouTube.

- Don't forget that while images will increase views on Facebook, videos will bring you even more engagement.

- Adding more than one image to a blog post will increase social shares.

In a post last year on Forbes, Jayson DeMers wrote:

"Content will demand more visual mediums. There are several reasons why visual content will continue to become more important. Wireless connections and Internet speeds continue to increase, giving people more capacity to access images and videos even while on the go. The written content market continues to become more saturated, leaving users with a higher demand for more visual forms of content. And users are becoming increasingly impatient, needing faster and more instant forms of communication. The result is a much higher demand for videos and other visual forms of content well into 2016."

Even video ads perform well. According to Digital Book World (DBW), Facebook is hitting the ball "out of the park" with its video ads. DBW also noted that Facebook users watch "100 million hours of video per day." In addition, "more than 500 million people watch Facebook video every day." In other words, videos are so powerful that people will even watch advertising in the form of video.

Don't worry, writers. You can overcome the aversion to blocks of black text by incorporating imagery into your blog and book marketing. Ready to boost your visual marketing? Here's how.

Add Images to Your Self-Hosted WordPress Blog

First a note: A self-hosted blog is one that you host on your WordPress website, not on WordPress.com.

Once you've written your blog post and added it to WordPress, click the Add Media icon, and then click Upload Files to add your blog graphic.

It's also here that you can decide to align the image, add a hyperlinked page, decide on a size for your image, or even add a caption if you'd like

After the upload is complete, focus on the right column of your media library. The title you used when you saved the image to your computer will display automatically. Now match the ALT Text to your image title, which should match your blog post title.

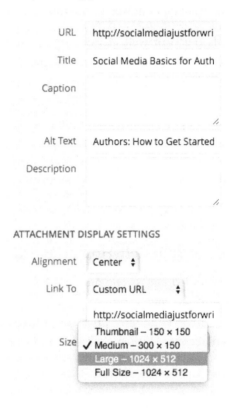

It's important to properly title your image. The name you assign to each image will appear on Pinterest and stay connected to the image on other social media. It's also a good idea to add an ALT Text to improve your search engine optimization. In addition, adding an Alt Text benefits the visually impaired. Screen readers, browsers that the visually impaired use, search for the ALT Text to inform the person using the computer about the contents of a picture.

To learn more about why Google likes you to include an ALT Text, refer to Google's Image Publishing Guide: https://support.google.com/webmasters/answer/114016?hl=en

Here's an example from Pinterest. The pinned image attaches my website address, to the picture and displays it along with the image title.

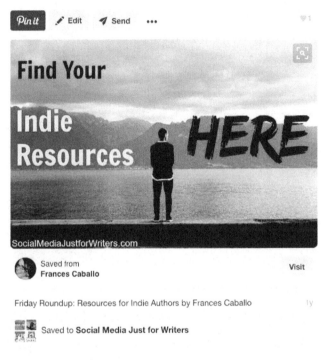

If you use Social Warfare as your social sharing icons, it will allow you to designate an image and a description for your saved images on Pinterest.

Use Images on Social Media

Images with quotes from your books is an excellent way to market your books and engage readers. Here's an example of dialogue as part of an image. Notice that the image includes a website address for branding.

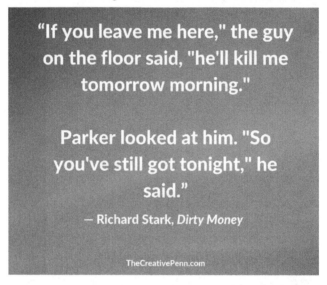

Readers also enjoy inspirational quotes.

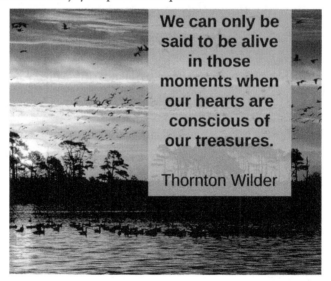

And book lovers might enjoy a collage of interesting bookshelves.

Use Multiple Images with Your Blog Posts

Do you, due to the pressure of time constraints, neglect to include images with your blog posts? As the statistics indicate, it's important to have at least one image with each post, and even better if you can include more than one.

Here's an example from my blog.

How to Create Images Using Canva

Canva.com is a free online, image-creation tool. The beauty of Canva is that its templates have the correct photo dimensions built in. What this means is that you won't need to look them up for each social media network. Plus, you can create images using unique dimensions, such as calls to action at the end of a blog post or elsewhere on your website.

Let's say that you want to create an image for a Facebook post. Select the Facebook template, select a background image or add the code for your brand color, and select a text template or one of Canva's free layouts.

Canva also provides text templates.

Canva also provides collage templates that you merely need to add your images to.

You can also purchase low-cost images from Canva or select free icons and grids from it's Elements store. Visuals you can create range from banners and header images for Facebook, Twitter, and YouTube, to business cards, letterhead, graphics for Tumblr, and even book covers.

To create a book cover, go to https://www.canva.com/create/book-covers. Select a photo with a template or upload your picture and decide how you want to organize the text on the cover. Within a few minutes, you have a new book cover.

There are other image creation tools on the web, some of which are free and some aren't.

- Use Easel.ly to create infographics. Easel.ly offers a free account and a pro account.

- Infogr.am is an infographic-creation tool. It's pricing starts at $19/month.

- Canva provides additional features on its paid account. Monthly billing is $12.95 or $119.40/annually, which works out to $9.95/month.

- PowToon is a fun way to create animated videos. This tool offers a free plan, but its pro plan is $89/month.

- With PicMokey, you can edit and crop photos, overlay words onto images, create Facebook banners, and mount images into a collage. You can pay $4.99/month or $33/year.

- BeFunky is a fun tool as well. Upload an image for free and start adding your creativity to it. You can crop it, resize it, rotate it, add a background, sharpen it, and more.

- Kanvas is a mobile tool for iPhone and Android users.

- Create collages on the go with Photo Grid. It's available as an app for iPhone and Android users.

- Tweetroot is an iPhone app that lets you create word clouds from your Twitter account.

- Pablo by Buffer is one of the easiest photo apps to use. Search one of Pablo's 600,000 royalty free images or upload one of your own. Then add text, adjust the contrast, and voila, you have an image to share on Facebook, Twitter, Instagram, or Pinterest.

- Piktochart, which costs $15/month, features more than 500 templates, images, icons, charts, and ready-to-use graphics to create professional images without the cost of hiring a designer.

- VideoScribe is a cool tool. Whiteboard-style animation videos are all the rage and this is the tool you need to use to create some for your blog or website.

Where to Find Royalty-Free Images

There are several online sources that say they provide free images but you need to be careful. Some of these free sites actually offer few free pictures. However, the online venues mentioned below do provide free pictures right now. When indicated, be sure to credit the photographer.

- Pixabay
- Negative Space
- Polar Fox
- Travel Coffee Book
- Pexels
- Morgue File
- Death to the Stock Photo
- Unsplash

Or you can go to LibreStock, where you can search 47 free stock photo websites in one venue.

Chapter 11
Popular Pinterest for Writers

Colors, like features, follow the changes of the emotions
Pablo Picasso

Picasso was hardly the starving artist in a garret. His artistic accomplishments brought him fame and great wealth in his lifetime. He was successful, in part, because he captured some of our most horrific moments and forced us to feel.

Pinterest will never suffer comparisons to Picasso, but when this social media darling—really a search engine, according to the founders—appeared on the virtual landscape, it caught our attention and left us entranced.

On this platform, we are swept away by captivating images, not lines of text. It's also revolutionary in its cataloguing of images and offers users a plethora of photographs, paintings, and quote images to behold. You'll find clothing to covet, books to read, and rules to writing.

Its growth has been exponential. Between September and December 2011, unique visitors to its website climbed by 429% and, as of this writing, Pinterest continues to be popular. Presently it has an estimated 100 million monthly active users but far more accounts. Users love to peruse images of crafts, do-it-yourself projects, and interior design. However, authors will use this network by uploading the covers to their books, their colleagues' books, and by creating pinboards that further their brand.

Pinterest is a social media venue Picasso would have toasted with a pitcher of sangría. Just imagine how he would have utilized it to spread his paintings and sculptures around the world. Art aficionados tucked into the valleys of Ireland or along the Mississippi River would have found his art virtually accessible and relevant if only social media had existed a century ago.

Picasso's fluctuating artistic expressions varied from his Blue Period to his Rose Period to Cubism and then to Surrealism. At every flick of the brush, he would have found fans and followers worldwide on Pinterest attracted to his styles. His ego, already healthy, might have swelled even more. Just like Picasso, you can change your style on Pinterest, experiment with boards of different themes, spur or support a revolution with your words and images, and become known from Bora Bora to Latvia. If you create a pinboard and a month later you detest it, rip it up virtually. If one pinboard loses its focus, use some of the images to create more pinboards. Create, edit, change, and revise.

Is your novel set in Spain? Create a pinboard of the places your characters travel to or where they live. Is your book about horses? Assemble a pinboard of beautiful horses from around the world. Did you write a book about grantwriting for nonprofits? Are you considering a new novel? Create some secret boards with the clothing and jewelry your characters might wear. Looking for writing prompts to kickstart your new chapter? Peruse more images on Pinterest. Do you write memoir? Upload some personal photographs. Do you promote your book with your blog? Hyperlink an image from your blog post and save it to Pinterest so that when users click on your image, they will immediately navigate directly to your blog. The possibilities are endless.

The Importance of Images

Researchers found that colored visuals increase people's willingness to read a piece of content by 80%. —James Mawhinney, HubSpot.com

What the above quote—and the research Mawhinney refers to—tells us is that if you don't use images in your marketing, you're making a mistake. Colored visuals improve engagement with your readers on social media, subsequent traffic to your website, and dedicated blog readers.

For example, if you write insightful blog posts, but you aren't incorporating images into the posts, you may be losing valuable readers who, over time, would purchase your books and retain you for any services you offer, such as editing.

In the same blog post, Mawhinney goes on to say,

> "Content with relevant images gets 94% more views than content without relevant images."

The importance of images is what makes Pinterest an essential part of your marketing. Publishers are increasingly using Pinterest to market their authors' books.

A Closer Look at Pinterest

One of the beauties of Pinterest is that you can save images from your website to a dedicated pinboard and subsequently enjoy increased traffic to your blog, website, or other landing pages when readers save (formerly "pin") the image and click on the website link.

Take a look at the people who are using Pinterest. (*Source: SproutSocial, February 2015)*

- As of February 2015, 71% of Pinterest's users were women.

- Men are a growing demographic on Pinterest. One-third of signups are now coming from men. ". . . more men use the platform in the U.S. every month than read *Sports Illustrated* and *GQ* combined."

- Pinterest is increasingly mobile. Seventy-five percent of Pinterest usage occurs on mobile devices. Forty-five percent of users are from outside the United States. (September 2015)

- Users are avid online shoppers.

- Pinterest is popular among Millennials.

Other sources indicate that its consumer base is international (think book sales in India), and that it has a broad consumer base of Millenials (those born between the early 1980s and the early 2000s).

Pinterest's growth is further substantiated by an August 2015 study by Pew Research Center. The study noted, "The proportion of online adults who use Pinterest and Instagram has doubled since Pew Research Center first started tracking social media platform adoption in 2012."

This last statistic substantiates the fact that visually based social media is key.

The most frequently visited images on Pinterest include these categories: home décor, DIY and crafts projects, and style and fashion. The top-visited boards make sense because two-thirds of the network's registered users are women.

How to Get Started

To get started on this network, go to www.Pinterest.com and sign up. Make sure that you sign up for a business account. Business accounts have access to free analytics, and you can have your website verified. (This involves asking your webmaster to insert a code on your website.) When you verify your website, your images will have a better chance of standing out in search results, and the verification lends credibility to your website.

Your username should be your author name. In other words, if you use a pseudonym, you need to use that name. Remember, you are your brand, so you need to use your complete name as it appears on your book covers.

When you describe yourself, include keywords. Whether your genre is romance, erotica, thriller, young adult, or another niche, make sure that you include your genre in your bio.

You'll need to include your website URL and upload a profile image. Pinterest will ask you whether you want to connect your account to Facebook and Twitter. Don't do this. It's never a good idea to sync one social media network with another. In the case of linking Pinterest to other social networks, those posts rarely trigger any engagement with readers.

The next step is to add the Browser Button to your browser taskbar so that you will be able to select and save photos that you find while searching the Internet or from your website or Amazon. You can't save images from Facebook, but you can do that with images on Twitter.

The process of adding the icon will depend on which browser you use. However, Pinterest provides easy-to-follow directions. To add the Browser Button, navigate to this web address: http://pinterest.com/about/goodies. If you need help, you'll find answers to your questions here: https://pinterest.com/about/help.

On Facebook you have friends and fans. On Twitter you have followers, and on LinkedIn you have connections. On Pinterest, you'll have followers. Here, you can follow other users, called pinners, or you can follow the boards that appeal to you.

Before creating pinboards, follow some of your writing colleagues and readers for a few days. Look at their boards, follow them, and let your ideas about the types of pinboards you want to create germinate.

You can start by creating pinboards for your favorite books, poets, or visual writing prompts. What if someone follows you and you like only one or two of their pinboards? Just follow the pinboards you like—a nice feature Pinterest offers.

Pinterest's Taskbar

Let's take a look at the top taskbar on Pinterest's website.

When you click the Pinterest logo at the far left, you'll navigate to the newsfeed. Here, you'll find all the images saved or shared by the people you follow.

Click Analytics to discover how many people are saving (similar to retweets) your images. Click Ads to create an ad.

Use the search bar to find images. Treat the search bar the same way you'd use Google's search bar. Are you looking for author quotes? Use those two keywords in the search bar.

When you click the series of lines to the right of the search bar, a dropdown menu of categories will appear.

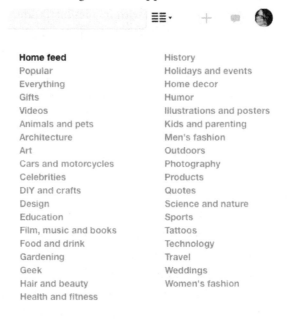

Home feed

Popular

Everything

Gifts

Videos

Animals and pets

Architecture

Art

Cars and motorcycles

Celebrities

DIY and crafts

Design

Education

Film, music and books

Food and drink

Gardening

Geek

Hair and beauty

Health and fitness

History

Holidays and events

Home decor

Humor

Illustrations and posters

Kids and parenting

Men's fashion

Outdoors

Photography

Products

Quotes

Science and nature

Sports

Tattoos

Technology

Travel

Weddings

Women's fashion

When you click the plus sign, you can save an image from your blog or website, upload an image from your computer, or create an ad.

Another drop-down menu appears when you click your picture on the far right. You can click My Profile to navigate to your pinboards, access your settings, look at bills from your advertising, request ad support, look for help, or log out.

Look for Images on Pinterest

Use the search bar to explore images by keywords. Maybe you want to create a pinboard that portrays the type of clothes your characters wear. Or maybe you're creating a pinboard of infographics related to your nonfiction books.

When you find a photo you like, click the like and save buttons. If you'd like, you can also click the send button, and send the image to a friend. If you email the picture to a friend, you'll need to add an email address. Pinterest will prompt you to add a message as well. The email your friend receives will look like this:

Frances Caballo **found a Pin for you!**

Take a closer look

Once you click save, Pinterest will give you the option to create a new board or save the photo to a board you already started. Don't forget to leave a comment. In the example below, I wrote this comment: "Great image for a writing prompt!" I could also leave an additional comment where it says at the bottom of this screenshot, "Add a comment."

Saved from
a1pictures.blogspot.ca   Visit

Great image for a writing prompt!

Frances Caballo

Saved to **Writer's Life**

Comments

Add a comment...

Categorize Your Images for SEO

Categorizing your pinboards is an important step in helping your images become discoverable on Pinterest. When you categorize your images, you'll increase the chances that other users will find your images, and thus links to your website.

Traffic to your website will increase when you "save" images from your blog, website, and other landing pages, such as a page dedicated to each of your books. Saving images from your website is part of a search engine optimization strategy you should use on a regular basis.

Here's an example. Select My Profile by clicking on your image in the taskbar and then select a board you've created. Open the pinboard and click Edit Board. You'll want to complete the sections in the image below, using keywords in your description. In this case, I made sure I used two keywords, *readers* and *authors*.

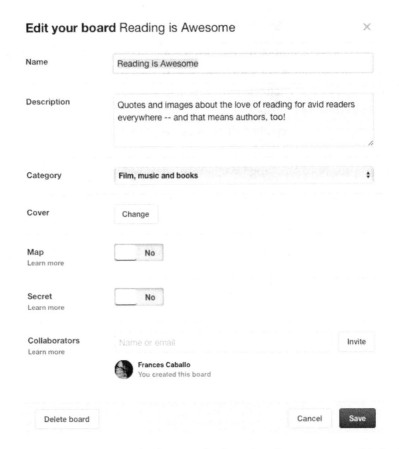

In the above case, I don't want the board to be a secret and I don't need the saved images to revolve around a geographic area. Let's say that you have a condo in Hawaii that you have available for vacation rental. In that case, you would want to add the map feature.

You might want to designate a pinboard as a secret in the following situations:

- You're uploading personal images to share sparingly with a few friends.

- You're collecting images that pertain to your next book. The board may be intended for research.

If you are displeased with the cover of your board, click Change. And if you'd like your board to be collaborative, enter the email addresses of your friends.

As a final note, you can also enhance the chance that your images will be discovered by:

- Including keywords in your account description.

- Opening a business account and verifying your website.

- Using keywords to assign names to your pinboards.

- Moving your boards with images from your blog and books to the top of your profile, so that other users will see them first.

- Using hashtags in your comments.

Pay Attention to Image Names and ALT Texts

You can also improve your pins' discoverability by how you name your images. For example, instead of naming an image BlogArt-1-1-16 when adding images to your blog for saving later, use keywords when you create the image. Then when you upload the visual to your blog, fill in the ALT Text.

For example, I created this image for a blog post about Goodreads. I used keywords in the image title and the Alt Text. The Alt Text, includes the keywords *Goodreads* and *authors.*

URL	http://socialmediajustforwriter
Title	How to Set Up Your Goodreads
Caption	
Alt Text	How to Set Up Your Goodreads
Description	
Uploaded By	Frances Caballo
Uploaded To	How to Set Up Your Goodreads Author Dashboard

Now you know how to set up your business account, save images from the web, and improve your SEO with Pinterest.

Pinboard Suggestions for Authors

Pinterest is a powerful referral source of traffic to your website, blog, and Amazon.

According to Mashable:

"When it comes to referral traffic from social networks, there's Facebook and Pinterest—and then there's everyone else."

The *Business Insider* added this comment to the discussion: "Pinterest drives 7.10% of Web traffic that sites receive, second only to Facebook (21.25%), and leagues ahead of other social sites like Twitter, Reddit,

StumbleUpon and LinkedIn. In the first quarter of 2014, the company drove 48.36% more traffic than it did at the end of 2013."

This research substantiates the fact that you need to create pinboards for the books and blog posts you write if you want increased traffic to your designated landing pages.

Pinterest and Your Blog

With the prospect of getting referral traffic to your website, it makes sense that you would take the time to create images or find images for your blog. Your image could lead to readers discovering your post, your website, and then your books. Before long, you have readers buying your books and, if you offer them, your services.

Take this image, for example. It was straightforward, yet it was my most popular shared image that week.

Hi there,

A great way to try Promoted Pins is to promote Pins that are already doing well. Select Pins that link back to your website where people can buy your products, subscribe to your updates or find out more.

This Pin drove the most traffic to your site this month:

When you create your first boards, make sure they are for your blog and book because whenever you save images from your website, blog or Amazon, the web address will attach to the picture. Then when other users save your image, they will have the option to travel to your website when they click one of a variety of messages that will appear in the lower, righthand corner. Those messages change and include Visit, Read It, or Make It.

In this example, the book cover leads to a blog post about nine books. Notice that the website is noted beneath the image.

In this example, the link at the lower right-hand corner changes to Read It. The page includes the source, and notes that this book received a Goodreads Choice Award.

BuzzFeed

The Best Books Of 2014, According To Goodreads Users

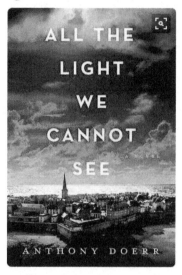

  Article from
BuzzFeed

Read it

The Goodreads Choice Awards are the only major book awards chosen by readers. And the readers have spoken!

If you write cookbooks, you might have a website where you share some of your recipes. In that case, the link at the lower righthand corner will change to Make It.

THE BEST GLUTEN-FREE
FUDGY BROWNIES
DAIRY-FREE + WHOLE GRAIN

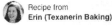

Recipe from
Erin (Texanerin Baking)   Make it

Pinboard Ideas for Authors

When I speak with authors about Pinterest, they are often perplexed about how to use this network. You can use these suggestions as a starting point for building your unique presence on Pinterest.

Fiction Author Pinboard Suggestions

- A pinboard for your blog images
- Quotes about reading
- Images of old and antique books
- A collection of your favorite books
- Quotes about the joy of reading

- Fun, funky, unusual bookstores
- Libraries from around the world
- Images of your favorite literary characters
- Humorous sayings about the life of writers
- Quotes from authors about life
- Writing advice for authors
- A collection of book covers from your colleagues
- Books by authors from your region or state
- Images of your favorite authors
- Examples of bookshelves and bookcases
- Images from your favorite writers conferences
- Pictures from author readings you've attended
- Visual writing prompts
- Images that portray the cities and countries where your characters live and travel to
- The type of clothing your characters wear
- Jewelry your characters wear or might wear
- Your characters' favorite meals
- Images you create using quotes from your books and favorite blog posts
- Images that reflect scenes in your next book
- Visuals from websites you'll use when you research your next book
- Historical characters or events you'd like to write about in subsequent historical fiction novels
- Quotes your characters would love
- Places your characters plan to travel to or dream about visiting

Don't hesitate to create pinboards just for fun that let your readers learn about your personal side.

Pinterest Suggestions for Romance/Erotica Authors

- Create a pinboard for all of your book covers
- A collection of sexy jewelry your characters wear
- Images of seductive clothing your characters might might wear
- A pinboard of dreamy picnic settings
- Pictures of shoes and dresses your characters would wear on a hot date
- Photos of actors and models you see as desirable and would like to emulate in future books
- Alluring hairstyles
- A collection of lingerie
- Pictures of lips, eyes, or legs
- Images of rich chocolate or champagne
- Images of your characters' favorite drinks
- Models or actors who inspire your writing
- All of your blog images
- Quotes from women about how they define sexy
- Quotes from men about how they define sexy
- Some of the suggestions above for fiction authors
- Pictures of sexy men or women reading

Pinboard Suggestions for Nonfiction Writers

- Pinboard of all your blog images
- Infographics
- Images from other bloggers you admire

- Images from blogs where you write guest posts

- Pinboards developed around your niche or niches

- If you write about diabetes, create a pinboard of recipes for diabetics.

- If you write about hiking, create pinboards for boots, hats, sunglasses, tents, trails, etc. Do the same for books on yoga, history, or productivity strategies.

- If you write about the importance of exercise, create pinboards of walking paths, workout routines, walking shoes, etc.

- Whatever your niche might be, create boards filled with images that inform your readers.

- Collect quotes that are informative and reflect your specialty.

- Use some of the suggestions above for fiction authors.

Pinboard Suggestions for Poets

- Collect images that provide you with visual inspiration for your writing.

- Photographs of beaches

- Pictures from your hikes into the woods

- Overlay favorite lines of your poetry on beautiful images

- Overlay favorite lines from your favorite poets on images

- Plan a pinboard of your favorite poets

- Book covers from your favorite poets

- Quotes that inspire you

- Images that captivate your imagination

- Any depictions of the natural environment that encourage you to write

Pinboards for Picture Book Authors and Illustrators

- Create a new pinboard for every book you write, and include all or most of your images

- Collect pictures of bedtime reading rituals

- Create visuals or collect images you find that portray the importance of reading to children

- Promote diversity in children's literature

- Pinboards of book covers about divorce and other issues.

- Images from your blog and elsewhere on your website

- Create images that reflect the topics you cover in your books. If you write about marine life, create pinboards of sea turtles, seashells, creatures of the sea, ocean beauties, dolphins, etc.

- Create pinboards of resources for teachers and parents

- Establish a pinboard that reflects the importance of literacy

- Build a board of book covers from the books your colleagues and editors write

Many of the suggestions for fiction authors can also apply to picture book authors, so be sure to review them as well.

Start using Pinterest today to complement your marketing and bring new traffic to your website and blog.

Chapter 12
How Authors Can Make the Most of Instagram

Taking pictures is savoring life intensely, every hundredth of a second.
Marc Riboud

According to a report by Digital Marketing Research, as of March 2016, Instagram had 400 million monthly active users and captured the attention of 20% of all Internet users.

Part of its growth might be due to the mother of all social media networks, Facebook. After Facebook purchased the app in 2014, Instagram's user base soared by 60%. (You can set up your Instagram advertising on Facebook when creating Facebook ads.) Then again, Instagram probably grew so quickly just because it's an image-based application and any social media network (such as Pinterest) based on imagery is bound to succeed these days.

Hard to tell.

There are conflicting reports as to which social media network is the fastest growing. The data seems to change from month to month, or at least, it did in 2015. That year, Adweek, TechCrunch, and Global Web Index each reported different statistics.

It was also in 2015 that Pew Research Center reported that Instagram was the fourth most used social media network, behind Facebook, LinkedIn, and Pinterest.

If your reader demographic is between the ages of 18 and 49, Instagram can be a strategic application for you to use. If you write young adult, new adult, dystopian, and teen and young adult romance and science fiction novels, then you need to spend time connecting with your readers on Instagram.

Some agents are recommending that all authors, including nonfiction writers with an older readership, also use Instagram. Perhaps it's because of Instagram's meteoric rise.

But if your audience isn't on Instagram, does it make sense to use it? I'm a huge proponent of saving time on social media by only spending time on those networks where you'll find your readers and your colleagues. But with Instagram's popularity, it might make sense for you to grab your username anyway. After doing that, play around with Instagram and see whether it's worthwhile for your genre and readership. If it isn't, leave Instagram, focus your energy on other websites, and return to it later to test it again.

The beauty of Instagram—and this is why it's easy to test it—is that it's effortless to incorporate it into your life. For now, let's leave the statistics behind and talk about how to sign up and use this tool.

How to Join Instagram

Profile Image
Joining this network is easy. Sign up by navigating to Instagram.com on your PC, Mac, smartphone, or tablet. It's best to use your smartphone because Instagram is for the mobile web. As with other social media websites, don't use your book cover or image of your favorite pet as your avatar. Use the best picture of yourself that you have.

Every time you add a new network to your marketing arsenal, represent your brand as best you can. What is your brand? You. Some writers become irritated at the mention of the term author brand but denying that it exists doesn't deny its importance. Everything you do and say online reflects upon you so every step you take online, every post, every image you upload, needs to support your author career in as positive a manner as possible.

Username

When you select your username, use the name on the cover of your books. Build your brand around your author name, whether it's your birth name, a name you predominantly use, or a pen name.

Bio

Complete your bio, which Instagram restricts to 150 characters, and add your author website address. Don't forget to check the box next to Similar Account Suggestions so that Instagram will suggest additional users for you to follow.

Desktop and Laptop Restrictions

You may be limited in what you can do from your desktop or laptop whether it's a PC, Mac, or laptop. You can sign up, complete your bio, follow people, view your news feed, like images, and leave comments.

Most people carry around their smartphones in their back pockets so start using your mobile phone when using Instagram. Alternatively, use your tablet if you bring that with you more often.

As you're out and about, visiting your favorite café where you write or taking a walk in the woods or on a lovely path, snap images with your smartphone. Then, upload them directly to Instagram. Select a filter for your image if the image appears too dark or too bright, and post it. Don't forget to add a few hashtags too.

Now this next step is what makes Instagram simple to use. As you post your image to Instagram, you can also post it to other accounts, including Facebook, Twitter, Tumblr, and Flickr. While I don't recommend syncing Twitter to Facebook or even Instagram to Twitter, linking Instagram to Facebook is seamless. The comment and hashtags you write for your Instagram post will integrate smoothly with your Facebook profile. This is how to connect your accounts:

1. Navigate to your Instagram profile on your smartphone.

2. Tap the gearshift in the top-right corner.

3. Click Linked Accounts and select the websites you want to sync with.

How Authors Can Use Instagram

Authors have taken to Instagram, expanding their brand, and letting readers learn about them. Check out these examples:

Tyler Knott Gregson

You'll find Tyler on Instagram where he's known as Tyler Knott, an #Instapoet on this app. He's a successful poet who rose to fame by using Instagram. He creates quote images and posts them mostly on Twitter and Instagram.

Here's one of his poems displayed as an image:

Jane Friedman

Jane was excited about the inclusion of an essay she wrote in an anthology and announced its availability with this picture of the cover. Granted, it's not an exciting cover, but it's still a good use of Instagram.

Orna Ross

Orna likes to take pictures of her surroundings, which gives her readers and colleagues a sense of the beauty where she lives in the U.K.

Joanna Penn

A nonfiction and dark thriller author who writes her fiction under the name J.F. Penn, Joanna is a self-described taphophiliac (she loves visiting cemeteries) so it makes sense that she would post this image.

Crissi Langwell

While attending attending an Indie author event at a library, Crissi took an image of a display of her books.

Share the cover of a new book about to be released, images from your hometown, or of the desk where you write. If you have a favorite café where you like to write, take a picture of the sign or the front of the building. If you love dogs, take a picture of your dog doing something fun. When you have a reading, ask someone to snap a picture of you, preferably not when you're standing behind a podium but during a moment when you're animated, laughing, or engaging with an attendee. Most of all test this app and have fun with it.

When to Post on Instagram

The easiest time to post is right after you take a picture or create one. You can also plan your posts.

According to Later, a scheduling application for Instagram, the best time to post is between 2 am (yes, 2 am!) and 5 pm EST, with 5 pm being the most opportune time. The best day to post is on Wednesdays, but if you start using Instagram, you'll need to be consistent and post more frequently than once a week.

When you start out, post images when it's convenient for you. As you gain followers, you'll figure out when the most engagement occurs and tailor your timing.

Scheduling Apps for Instagram

Once you start using Instagram regularly, you might want the option to schedule images in advance.

Onlypult
With this app, you can upload images and videos from your computer, not just your smartphone. Onlypult also provides analytics. Plans start at $12/month.

Later
This tool enables you to upload images from your computer, iPhone, Tablet, or Android, plan and schedule your posts, upload videos and manage multiple accounts if you have more than one. On a free account, you can upload 30 posts per month.

Schedugram
With this tool, you can organize campaigns or schedule images one-by-one, manage multiple accounts, create content, and add bulk uploads at once. For a single account, the cost is $20/month.

Takeoff
Use this free app to schedule images to Twitter and Instagram simultaneously. You'll find it on iTunes and at Google Play where it's called Publish.

Instagram Best Practices

Here are a few best practices to get you started.

1. Use hashtags here just as you would on Twitter. Although hashtags haven't taken off on Facebook, they're important on Instagram.

2. Don't be afraid to reveal a bit about your personal life. Images you take while hiking or cycling or just around town add an interesting layer to your brand.

3. Always be authentic.

4. Don't be promotional, unless you'd like to inform users of a contest.

5. Build your community of readers and colleagues by liking their posts and commenting on them. Be as engaged with them as you'd like them to be with you.

Chapter 13
Snapchat:
The Fun Social Media Network
that Millenials Dominate

Somewhere along the way, when we were building social media products,
we forgot the reason we like to communicate with our friends is because it's fun.
Snapchat CEO Evan Spiegel

Life's more fun when you live in the moment.
Snapchat slogan

Social media aficionados like to jump on the newest, shiniest objects on the Internet and there are few sites attracting more buzz than Snapchat.

Bloomberg Technology reported in June 2016 that Snapchat had 150 million daily users. To put this number in perspective, that means that Snapchat now exceeds Twitter in daily users. (Twitter has 110 million daily users.)

An estimated 60% of Snapchat's users visit the app to create images and videos. Major brands that market to young adults and millennials are using this app to promote their wares. Buzzfeed, MTV, and Tastemade offer stories on Snapchat—and so do CNN and The Wall Street Journal.

If you're wondering what Snapchat is, let me begin again. Quite simply it's an image and video messaging application. It's similar to

WhatsApp, another messaging app, except that Snapchat's messages are temporary (they vanish) in nature, and it supports two-way video messaging, similar to Skype but not as stodgy.

Snapchat is not for every writer, but if you're an author of teen, young adult, or new adult fiction, then you'll want to consider it. There are also a fair amount of romance writers on Snapchat.

Consider these statistics from the Business Insider:

- The majority of its users are female and between of 13 and 25.

- Two-fifths of 18-year-olds in the U.S. use it several times a day to check in with friends and some family members.

Marketing Dive offers an expanded view:

- In 2015, Snapchat grew its 18-24-year-old base by 56%, while its 25-34-year-old users increased 103%.

- Older snappers are joining the site as well. According to com-Score, the over-35 user base grew by 84% last year.

- According to Snapchat, 12% of its almost 50 million daily users in the U.S. are between 35 and 54.

In 2015, Business Insider reported that according to a Comscore analysis, there are more millennials on Snapchat than any other social media platform. The vast majority of the millennial users are between 18 and 25 years of age.

Signing Up for Snapchat

If Snapchat intrigues you, go to your mobile phone and download the app to get started. You'll need a username and password. Some bloggers recommend using a fun name. If you're a teen, sure, pick a hilarious name your friends will like. But if you're an author, use the name that appears on your book covers.

Once you sign up, you'll need to confirm your email. Soon you'll receive a series of fun, informative images and Team Snapchat will send you a video of instructions on how to use the app.

What can you do with Snapchat? Quite a bit!

snap   chat   video chat

add a doodle   tell stories   keep up
or caption   with friends

watch   ...as if you   discover
live events   were there!   more to
                                 discover

happy snapping!
TEAM SNAPCHAT

To add your profile image, tap on the ghost. You can stay in one position or move your head around to create a GIF avatar. (A GIF is an animated image.)

To revise your settings, click on the gearshift. Here you can:

1. Change your password

2. Change your email

3. Set up your login verification

4. Decide whether your want to be notified of incoming Snaps by a ring or sounds.

5. View your friend emojis (a small digital image or icon use to express an idea or emotion) and filters. (To use a filter, swipe left once you take an image.)

6. Decide who can contact you

7. Determine who can view your stories (stories are a collection of images or snaps)

8. Contact support

9. Review the privacy policy

10. Clear your browser data and conversations

11. Block users

12. Log out

Snapchat's Chap 2.0 release added video chat, video, audio notes, and stickers to the platform. Video views are popular. Presently, Snapchat users generate 10 billion daily video views.

Snapchat Lexicon

Every social media website has its own vernacular and Snapchat isn't any different. Here's a list of terms to be aware of.

- **Snaps** are photos and videos. After a friend views a snap, it self-destructs, meaning it vanishes forever unless you create a screenshot of it.

- **Filters:** You can overlay one of several filters on images you take.

- **Stories** are collections of snaps that last up to 24 hours.

- If you were to swipe up from the bottom of the screen while reading a story, you can reply to the user.

- **Snap Score:** This is the total number of snaps you have sent and received, which shows up next to your name.

- **Snapstreak:** When you send messages to the same friends several days in a row, you are officially on a Snapstreak.

- **Discover:** This is probably where you'll end up going first to better understand Snapchat content. The Discover tab lists a variety of brands, including ESPN, Food Network, BuzzFeed, People Magazine, Mashable, Cosmopolitan, the Wall Street Journal and others. Just swipe from left to right to view the brand's stories and select one to read by tapping on an image.

- **Chat:** To start a chat, swipe right a user's name. Chat messages disappear once you've read them.

- **Geofilters:** A geofilter is an overlay on an image you took in a specific geographic area. If you want to create a geofilter for where you're living or visiting, take a picture or record a video and swipe across the screen. You'll see available geofilters for that area.

As with most social media sites, each time you visit the app, there's a newsfeed of updates and stories from the people or brands you follow.

When you're in messaging mode (which is similar to using an instant messaging app), you can click the image icon to access your camera roll, take a picture of yourself, hit the video icon to video conference with a friend or follower, or send a sticker.

As a test, I contacted Smashwords' founder Mark Coker. I'm sure he has better things to do than reply to a Snapchat test message from someone he doesn't know but hey, it's all in good fun. He responded right away with, "Hey." A week later he sent me another message. By the way, his Snap Score is 3,202.

Who's on Snapchat?

Here's a sample listing of just a few authors, bloggers, and publishers on Snapchat.

- Jane Friedman
- Mark Coker
- Nick Stephenson
- Martha Sweeney
- Stephanie Taylor
- The Graduated Bookworm
- Angeline M. Bishop
- Donna Hup
- Riverhead Books
- Alfred A. Knopf
- Crown Publishing
- Frances Caballo
- Kate Tilton
- John Green

Snapchat Posting Tips

Here are some general tips to get you started.

1. Want to grow a following on Snapchat? I've noticed people using their Snapchat avatar as their Twitter avatar and including a call to action to attract new followers to Snapchat.

2. Snapchat thrives on original content. Try not to repurpose images here. Create original videos just for this app.

3. Create stories of several snaps you create.

4. As with all social media, engage with your followers and readers. And engage with other authors.

5. Use filters on your photos.

6. Add text to your images by using Canva.com. Your dimensions will be 1080 pixels wide by 1920 pixels tall.

7. Introduce promotions, contests, and other perks for your readers.

8. Involve readers in your stories.

What are people doing on Snapchat? Here are a few examples:

- **Stephanie Taylor** offers tips on publishing.

- **Crown Publishing** created short videos—a couple of seconds each—of its authors showing their latest book.

- **The Graduated Bookworm,** who is a book blogger on BlogSpot, took a picture of a bag of books she recently purchased. (She doesn't reveal her name on her social media profiles except for her first name and the first initial of her last name, Morgan A.)

- **Mark Coker** uses Snapchat to send pictures. I asked him if he uses Snapchat to promote Smashwords authors and he replied, "I can."

- **Chloe Okoli** told me, "I haven't used Snapchat as much as I thought I would so I don't have much to say on how I use it for author purposes."

Angeline M. Bishop sent me the longest response to my query. She writes New Adult novels and is an active Snapchat user. She said this during a chat, "Snapchat is a great way for readers to see behind the velvet rope. Authors have a mystique about themselves and we are generally very private people. Snapchat helps readers see who their favorite authors are and helps them discover writers.

"I like to engage my readership and take part in things they are doing. The New Adult genre is exactly what the average Snap likes to read and college campus life is big on Snapchat.

"There's also a network of wonderful marketers here. They help you connect with your readership and encourage you to get to know the other Snapchat personalities. My advice to other authors would be … to think of Snapchat as a fun pool party. You get a chance to peek into someone's life and socialize for a moment. Don't take yourself too seriously, have fun, and comment on the things you find interesting."

Riverhead Books promoted books by its writers by creating a series of images and publishing them as a story. Here's one of them:

Here's a picture of a bag of books that the Graduated Bookworm posted.

Except for the short videos of authors holding their books that Crown Publishing posted, I didn't see any overt marketing. What I did find were authors giving their readers an inside view into an author's life. I found everything from Stephanie Taylor's son sleeping to images of Obama.

Stephanie Taylor shared a precious video that reveals the life of the author as a mom.

Angeline likes a certain phrase from President Obama's commencement address and shared it with her followers.

Stephanie Taylor shares her preference for a cold cup of java with plenty of whipped cream on top.

Angeline M. Bishop shares her appreciation for The Game of Thrones while letting readers know that she's too tired to watch it tonight.

Snapchat can be tough to get the hang of so follow people, snap some fun images, and enjoy your experience.

Chapter 14
How Authors Can Use Tumblr to Reach Younger Readers

We all live in virtual environments, defined by our ideas.
Michael Crichton, Author

Tumblr is a microblogging and social networking website that David Karp founded in February 2007. You can use this site as a blogging site or as a venue for your images, poetry, and blog posts.

As of October 1, 2016, Tumblr hosted more than 316.2 million blogs. There are 550 million monthly users, 280.4 million blogs, and 129.7 billion posts according to a company that tracks social media statistics, DMR. Forty-two percent of Tumblr's traffic is from the U.S.

Tumblr is most popular with the 18-to-29 year-old age bracket. About 13% of this demographic have used the site while 66% of all visitors are under the age of 35. Thirty-nine percent of users are under 25 years of age.

I may know what you're thinking right now. These days when everyone is talking about Facebook Live, Snapchat, and Instagram, isn't Tumblr sort of, well, passé?

Au contraire.

When Pew Research Center came out with its newest mobile messaging and social media study last August, the data-rich website revealed these demographics about Tumblr:

- One-in-ten online adults (10%) use Tumblr, a slight increase from the 6% who did so the last time Pew Research asked in December 2012.

- Black and Hispanic adults (15% respectively) are slightly more likely than white adults (9%) to be on Tumblr.

Sure, Tumblr isn't growing leaps and bounds like Instagram and Snapchat, but it's still a popular social media network that some authors might want to spend some time using.

Specifically, if you write young adult/new adult novels or if you write novels that young adults are snapping up, such as graphic novels, then Tumblr might be one of the social media websites that you incorporate into your marketing plan.

And if you're a poet, you'll find plenty of colleagues on this visual blogging site.

Authors and Author Services on Tumblr

There are a lot of writers on Tumblr, including:

- John Green, *The Fault in Our Stars* (John Green has several accounts, including John Green Books, John Green Quotes, A Daily Shot of John Green)

- Leigh Stein, *Dispatch from the Future*

- Rosecrans Baldwin, *Paris I Love You but You're Bringing Me Down*

- Jami Attenberg, *The Middlesteins*

- Emma Straub, *The Vacationers*

- Jane Friedman, *Publishing 101: A First-Time Author's Guide to Getting Published, Marketing and Promoting Your Book, and Building a Successful Career*

- Lang Laev, poet

- Neil Gaiman, *Fragile Things*

- Malinda Lo, *Ash*

Check out this list of services for and about authors that are also on Tumblr:

- NPR Fresh Air

- Readers Writers Journal

- Bookworks

- Bublish

- NaNoWriMo

There are also some publishing houses on Tumblr:
- Random House

- HarperCollins

- Chronicle Books

- Scribner Books

You'll also find bookstores on Tumblr (London Books, Book Passage in Northern California, and others) a blog devoted to writing prompts, (http://writingprompts.tumblr.com) and a comprehensive directory of YA authors (http://yahighway.tumblr.com/YAdirectory) on Tumblr. And Huffington Post Books is on Tumblr as well.

How to Sign Up for Tumblr

Signing up for Tumblr is straightforward. Go to Tumblr.com and use your author name when setting up your account. Complete your bio and add the same avatar that you use on other social media networks.

Now it's time to think about branding. In this example, I use the same color for my name and bio that I use on my website and my logo.

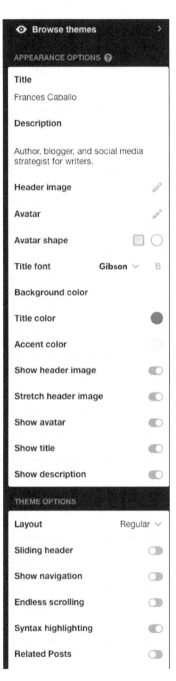

The next step is to select a theme, which you can do here (https://www.tumblr.com/themes/). The beauty and attraction of Tumblr, especially among teens and young adults, is the ability to customize your blog. Select one that matches your author brand. You can learn more about customization from Tumblr here (https://www.tumblr.com/docs/en/blog_customization).

If you don't want to purchase a theme—most cost about $49—you'll find numerous choices for customizing your account. Once you click Edit Theme, you'll see this long menu on the left-hand column: ➜

Next, follow some of your colleagues or some of the accounts mentioned above. Similar to Twitter, on Tumblr you have followers and you follow other users. Follow and unfollow with a simple toggle.

At the bottom of each of your followers' posts, you'll see these icons:

1. The left arrow allows you to send a post to someone you follow on Tumblr.

2. The balloon enables you to leave a comment.

3. The double arrow, similar to the retweet icon on Twitter, means you want to reblog a post on Tumblr. When you reblog, you can add a caption and tags. Tags are keywords and are referred to as hashtags on Twitter, Facebook, Instagram, and Google+.

4. The heart means that you like a post.

Don't Sync Facebook, Twitter, and Tumblr

You'll have the option to connect your Facebook and Twitter accounts to Tumblr. Doing this will save time but I don't endorse connecting these accounts. Each platform has its own voice and way of being in the virtual world of social media.

As a caveat, I do like the way Instagram users can decide, as they post an image, whether they want to also post it on Facebook. But to automatically post everything from one platform to another, well, as a practice I don't endorse it.

Ask Me Anything

When you set up your account, you can decide whether you want other users to contact you with questions. I like this option, so I've enabled it. What I won't enable, however, are anonymous questions.

Privacy on Tumblr

Be sure to indicate that you'd like your blog to be discoverable via search engines.

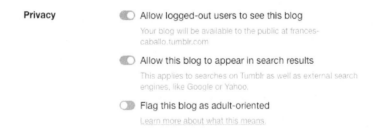

What to Post on Tumblr

As the above icons indicate, you can post blogs, images, quotes, links to blog posts, podcasts, videos, or chat with followers. So there are a lot of ways you can use this blogging platform.

Once you're on Tumblr, you can repost your best blog posts here. But as with other social media sites, images are huge. It would be better to create great images for your blog posts and then share the visuals to Tumblr and add the link to your post with a comment about it. Be sure to add tags before finalizing your post.

You can also create images just for Tumblr, such as quotes from your books, favorite author quotes, quotes about reading, books, libraries, etc.

If you use Canva, you'll see that the photo creation tool has a template for Tumblr images and has some ready-made suggestions for you.

Do you have a book video? Add it to Tumblr. Or did you create a how-to video your readers would enjoy? Add that too.

As with any social media platform, the possibilities are nearly endless.

Chapter 15
Meet Goodreads,
the Readers Haven

Goodreads has become the most important networking site on the Internet . . .
Forbes

The main reason the founders of Goodreads started this website was to create an online venue where friends could chat about and recommend books, the same way they might if they were dining together or meeting at a café.

Its secondary goal was to serve as a social media network. Users can even link their accounts to Facebook and Twitter to further spread the word about books they liked and reviewed.

Actually, on Goodreads, you can share a number of items, including

- Your book reviews.

- Information about books you've recently read and those on your to-read list through virtual bookshelves.

- Blog posts.

- Favorite quotes.

If you don't already belong to a book group in the city where you live, you can find one here, and it won't require you to leave your home or provide refreshments. Similar to a regular book group, you can share your insights, thoughts, and love of reading right from your home office or kitchen table.

You see, at its core Goodreads is all about the reader, not about using this platform to hawk your books. If you intend to start a Goodreads account for the purpose of merely acquiring friends and selling more books, you won't succeed. And you might even be mocked.

For example, if you try to rack up a high number of friends, like some writers do on various social networks, you might encounter a few unkind remarks. More than one reader warns writers looking for Goodreads followers, "If you're a self-published author wanting me to read your book, don't bother."

Ouch! Right? It's a harsh comment and one that you'll find if you don't take a strategic approaching to using Goodreads. While you'll occasionally find similar comments on this website, that shouldn't deter you from joining.

Goodreads' History

Goodreads launched in January 2007 by Otis Chandler (Founder, CEO, and the software engineer who developed it) and his wife, co-founder and editor-in-chief, Elizabeth Chandler. The idea of developing the site came as an epiphany to the founder one evening. (Source, Goodreads blog)

> One afternoon while I was scanning a friend's bookshelf for ideas, it struck me: when I want to know what books to read, I'd rather turn to a friend than any random person or bestseller list.
>
> So I decided to build a website—a place where I could see my friends' bookshelves and learn about what they thought of all their books.

And so Goodreads began.

On Goodreads you can see what your friends are reading, and they can find out what you're reading, want to read, and have read. You can create virtual bookshelves to organize your books (not the books you've written). You can read and comment on another reader's reviews, and explore new genres and discover new authors.

Goodreads even has an algorithm, not unlike the one Netflix and Amazon use. The algorithm examines prior ratings and books you read to sort through and find new books you might consider next. It's the perfect idea for avid readers.

To succeed—however you'd like to define success—you must first be an avid, active reader. Don't worry about generating book sales through Goodreads. Write the best book you can and readers, here and elsewhere, will find you.

Interesting Stats and Facts

As of January 2016, Goodreads had 50 million members, 1.3 billion books, and 47 million reviews.

In terms of demographics, Goodreads reports these numbers for 2014:

- Women read twice as many books as men.

- Men were twice as likely to write a 500+ page book.

- 80% of a female author's audience will be women.

- 50% of a male author's audience will be women.

- Women seem to express a slight preference for—according to their ratings—books written by women.

You'll find additional information here.

In 2013 Amazon purchased Goodreads. With Amazon taking over Goodreads, mainstream authors joined, including Stephen King and Khaled Hosseini.

Quantcast provides these statistics for the 30 days occurring between 11/30/15 and 12/29/15. Consider these numbers for just that month:

- Goodreads had 41.4 million global unique website visits; of those, slightly more came from outside the United States. (The unique website visit number doesn't include multiple visits from any one user.)

- Goodreads attracted 250.5 million global views.
- The gender demographic trended in favor of women.
- The 18–24 demographic was the largest, although there were sizeable numbers in the 25–44 age group.
- Many of its users attended college and even more attended graduate school.

If you're wondering which books fare well on this site, in the Goodreads' Choice Awards in 2015, the winners ranged from Harper Lee's *Go Set a Watchman* (fiction category) to *Girl on the Train* (mystery and thriller), to *The Nightingale* (historical fiction). The debut Goodreads author that year was Vitoria Aveyard, author of *Red Queen*, a young adult novel that made the New York Times best-seller list. An estimated 1.9 million Goodreads users voted for the Choice Awards winners.

Readers arrive at the virtual steps of Goodreads eager to share their critiques, participate in a group or two, and find their next great read. They read voraciously, love books as much as Hermione, and consume books of every genre. Enter the world of Goodreads knowing that if you can't match their passion for reading, your time might be better spent on Twitter or writing your next book.

How to Get Started

You are about to enter a world of avid book readers. Share your love for the written word by following the steps below.

Open An Account

If you are new to Goodreads, get started by navigating to www.goodreads.com. You can sign up either by signing in with your Facebook, Twitter, Google+, or Amazon accounts. Or, you can enter your name, email address, and a password.

It's Time to Add Books to Your Bookshelves

In the search bar, type the names of the books you want to read, have read, or are reading. If you can't find the book by its title, use the ISBN or author's name.

Let's say that you want to read *The Nightingale*. After typing the book title, click the green bar that says Want to Read.

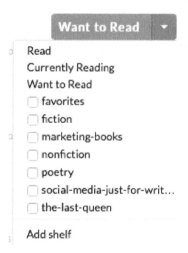

When you click on the arrow, you can see several options. You can separate your books by category, create a new shelf, and note a reading status such as Want to Read, Currently Reading, or Read.

Repeat this process until you've created several bookshelves.

Once you've finished reading a book you previously identified as Want to Read, simply click My Books in the top taskbar, navigate to the book you just finished, and click edit. You'll now be able to add the book to your shelf of books you've read.

choose shelves...   clos

○ read

○ currently-reading

◉ to-read

☐ favorites

☑ fiction

☐ marketing-books

☐ nonfiction

☐ poetry

☐ social-media-just-for-writers

Add new shelf

How can you update the status of a book you've been reading? Follow these steps:

1. Navigate to Home, which serves as a newsfeed. Here you'll see what all of your friends are reading or have read, and find links to their reviews.

2. Look at the right column and you'll see a widget noting the book you're currently reading. In this widget, you can update your reading status, add a new book you want to read or have read, or add a general update for your friends.

CURRENTLY READING

Business For Authors. How To Be An Author En
started on January 05, 2016   update status

I'm on page 0   of 310. –or– I'm finished!

[Save Progress]   Cancel

add a new book   add a general update

[post update]   Cancel

Compare Books

Have you wondered which books other authors like to read? Search for a
friend, and then click on that person's friends list. You will then navigate
to a list of friends and have the option to compare the books they've
read. In this example, I'm interested in learning what books author and
editor Jordan Rosenfeld has read. Just click on the green link, Compare
Books.

Jordan E. Rosenfeld
240 books | 2,374 friends
Morgan Hill, CA

Currently reading:
A Life in Men: A Novel
— Dec 22, 2014 11:07AM

Following

Jordan is your friend
compare books

The graphic demonstrates whether we are aligned in our tastes and then will list, one-by-one, books that Jordan has read but I haven't.

Jordan > Compare Books

▪ Jordan's books: 240 (238 not in common)
▪ Books in common: 2 (1.85% of your library and 0.83% of her library)
▪ My books: 108 (106 not in common)

Your tastes are 75% similar for the books you both rated.

sort   inverse popularity ⟳ ⒤

book title	Jordan's rating	my rating
Conundrum by C.S. Lakin	★★★★★	★★★★
The Orphan Master's Son by Adam Johnson	to-read	★★★★★

See what other books you have in common with Jordan. Rate each book you've read, or click "skip".

1. rate this book: ★★★★★ or skip

Reading Water: Lessons From The River (Capital Discoveries) by Rebecca Lawton

Jordan rated it: ★★★★★
bookshelves: favorites,

Enter the Goodreads Reading Challenge

Farther down in the same column on the Home Tab, you'll find the Goodreads reading challenge of the year. You can enter it by simply entering the number of books you want to read in a year.

2016 READING CHALLENGE

Challenge yourself this year!

I want to read ____ books in 2016.

Start Challenge

If you'd like to see how many books your friends anticipate reading in the year, click the 2016 Reading Challenge badge and you'll arrive at a page dedicated to the challenge. For example, in the 2016 Reading Challenge, by January 4th, 664,632 users pledged to read 32,527,716 books. By comparison, in 2015, 1.7 million Goodreads members completed 95 million books. The average reader had promised to complete 54 books that year.

A Review of Goodreads' Tabs

goodreads · Title / Author / ISBN · Home My Books Groups Recommendations Explore

To the right of the word *Goodreads* in the top taskbar, you'll find the search bar where you can enter book titles, authors, or ISBNs to find the books you want to read or review.

The Home tab is your newsfeed, where you'll find your friends' updates and have opportunities to update your books or enter the reading challenge.

The MyBooks tab lists the books you've read or are reading. The column to the left of your books has tools you can use.

tools

recommendations
add Amazon book purchases
widgets
import/export
find duplicates
shelf cloud
most read authors
stats
api

When you click Recommendations, you'll find books that the Goodreads algorithm thinks you'll enjoy based on your reading history. To improve recommendations for you, follow these steps:

1. Read and rate books throughout the year. If you subscribe to Netflix, you know that the website encourages its users to rate as many movies as possible to improve its recommendations for you. The same is true on Goodreads.

2. Create customized bookshelves. For example, instead of having two bookshelves for fiction and nonfiction books, create genre-related bookshelves for literary fiction, historical fiction, young adult, memoir, history, etc.

3. When Goodreads recommends books for you, follow the Netflix custom of indicating that you're not interested in some of Goodreads' recommendations.

Once you click Add Amazon Book Purchases, all of the books you buy through Amazon will appear on Goodreads.

Widgets have HTML coding. You can add these widgets to your website to share your reading lists with your website visitors.

Import/Export refers to reading lists you can import from your computer.

Have you entered the same book more than once? The Find Duplicates link will show these books to you so you can delete the duplicate listings.

The Shelf Cloud provides an interesting graph. Here you'll visually see which genres you prefer.

Which authors do you read the most? You'll find out by clicking Most Read Authors.

If you want to see a graph of the number of books you've read by year since joining Goodreads, click Stats.

The API tab leads to a special page for developers wanting to access Goodreads data.

Find Friends

You'll want to look for your friends. Click on the two-person icon to the left of your image on the top taskbar. Then click one of the icons in the

Find Friends From widget, or type in the name of a colleague or friend and search for friends one-by-one.

FIND FRIENDS FROM

M Gmail   Y7 Yahoo   f Facebook
Twitter
g Friends of friends

find by name or email | **search members** |

Goodreads gives users the opportunity to add a challenge question to their profiles. If you select this option, then prospective friends will need to know the correct answer to your question. I recommend that you don't take this step because you will limit your number of friends and potential readers of your books.

Goodreads also provides users with an option to exclude posts from your update feed. Here are the directions, quoted directly from Goodreads:

An easy way to exclude certain people from your feeds is to make a "top friends" list. This way, you can put all the people whose updates you would like to see in one place, separate from the people whose updates don't interest you. Then you can edit your feed to display only the updates from your top friends.

To do this

- *Click on the "Friends" icon in the header (it's the closest one to your profile pic).*

- *Click "edit friends" on the top of the page.*

- *Select the checkboxes of the people whose updates you would like to see as "top friends."*

- *Go back to the home page.*

- *Directly underneath the "updates" tab, there is an option that says, "showing: friends and people I'm following." Click the arrow to the right to display the list of settings.*

- *Select the radio button for "top friends" underneath the "From People" column on the right.*

- *Click the "apply filters" button.*

I think this option would limit your ability to find deeper connections with people you don't immediately know, but with whom you might unexpectedly find shared interests in books.

Books You've Read

When you enter a book you've read, you'll find that Goodreads automatically leads you to a page that lists

- the official product information.

- rating details.

- number of reviews.

- reviews by friends who have also read the book along with their ratings.

On this page, you'll find recommendations for books in the same genre that other readers enjoyed. And of course, there are links to Amazon where you can purchase the book as well as options to purchase it at other online venues or borrow it from your library. To add your local library to the links that appear beneath a book you want to read, follow these steps:

1. Click the arrow next to your image on the top taskbar.

2. Click Edit Profile.

3. You'll arrive at a new page with tab headings. Click Book Links.

4. On the right you'll find a green link that says Add A New Link. This is where you add your local library.

5. Next, customize the links you want to appear beneath books you're interested in. The example here shows the Sonoma County Library as at the top.

Sonoma County Library ▲▼ remove
iBooks   ▲▼ remove
Smashwords.com   ▲▼ remove
Libraries   ▲▼ remove
Indigo   ▲▼ remove
Abebooks   ▲▼ remove
Half.com   ▲▼ remove
Audible   ▲▼ remove
Alibris   ▲▼ remove
Better World Books   ▲▼ remove
IndieBound   ▲▼ remove
Amazon   ▲▼ remove
Shelfari   ▲▼ remove

About Book Links

Book links appear on all our book pages, where it says "find at". They let you find the book you're seeing at your favorite online book store, or any site that lets you search by ISBN in a URL.

Book links are intended to link to sites that have an ISBN search and have a large catalogue of books (booksellers, libraries, etc). Book links are not intended to link to sites about a particular book — those are best placed in the "url" or "description" field of the book.

Remaining Tabs

When you click the arrow to the right of the Explore tab, you'll find numerous links you can click. You can

- find books by genre.
- discover book giveaways.
- check out quizzes and quotes.
- see a list of Goodreads members who are currently online.

You'll also find Listopia when you click the arrow next to Explore. Here you'll find categorized books, such as featured lists of books, lists of books with recent activity, lists your friends voted on, and lists of the most popular books.

Once you're on the Listopia page, you can see a variety of links in the righthand column, including the ability to create your list. Click Create New List, and complete the information in the widget that appears.

search lists   **search**

Create New List
All Lists
Lists I Created
Lists I've Voted On
Lists I've Liked

Create A List

A listopia list is an ordered collection of books voted on by the community.

Title

Description

Tags

Save

The G in the top taskbar will take you to your news feed, also called Home. The envelope represents your inbox, and the two-person icon will list friend requests you receive that are waiting for your approval.

Link to Your Social Media

You can sync your social media accounts, including Twitter and Facebook. For example, Goodreads won't publish your tweets or status updates; the syncing is to link your activities on Goodreads to Twitter or Facebook, such as books you've completed reading or your recommendations.

To sync Goodreads to various accounts, click on the arrow next to your image in the top taskbar, and then click on *edit profile* and navigate to the *apps tab*.

You will then land on a page where you can link to the following websites:

- Facebook
- Twitter
- Google
- Amazon
- your eReader
- the Apple Store
- Google Play
- Blogger
- WordPress

If you review books on your blog, you can click a link to automatically export your Goodreads reviews to Blogger or to your WordPress blog.

Before you start syncing your accounts, consider how much automation you want. Maybe instead of syncing your accounts, you would rather write a tweet or Facebook update that includes the cover of the book. Also, consider the fact that Facebook downgrades synced status updates, so your update's visibility will likely be weak in your friends' newsfeeds.

Depending on how quickly you read and review books, you might want to link Goodreads to your Twitter account. If you're a book reviewer, you can add widgets to your website from Goodreads and link more accounts. If you write fiction, and your blog consists of reviews, you might want to sync more accounts.

The syncing and widgets enable Goodreads to expand its reach as part of its marketing effort. I'm not saying that syncing is a bad thing; I am pointing out that you'll want to sync thoughtfully the accounts that make sense for you, your brand, and the message you want to convey on your website, blog, and social media.

Helpful Links

If you have questions for the staff of Goodreads, this is how you can contact them.

Ask a question here: https://www.goodreads.com/about/contact_us

Learn more about advertising here: https://www.goodreads.com/advertisers

Find out about the author program: https://www.goodreads.com/author/program

Here's a link to the Goodreads help page: https://www.goodreads.com/help

In the next chapter, I'll share with you how to create your author account and use Goodreads to increase awareness of books you write.

Chapter 16
How to Set Up Your Goodreads Author Dashboard

Are you enjoying Goodreads so far? I hope so.

Now that you have a Goodreads profile, you can set up an author account. Your first step will be to search for your books. Follow the steps below.

How to Find and List Your Books

Go to the search bar and use your book's ISBN. If you don't have an ISBN, use your book title. Goodreads may not recognize the title if you haven't yet uploaded your book to Amazon. In that case, click Manually Add a Book. You'll find the link in green lettering in the right column.

Search

Manually add a book
Import books

| Social Media Time Suck | | Search |

Once you click Manually Add a Book, you'll arrive at a blank form. Here you'll need to add the title, author name, ISBN (ISBN 13 or ASIN), your book cover, and other details including your back cover description.

Claim your author profile, and add a photo of yourself as well as a bio and website URL. It's also a good idea to sync your blog or your RSS feed from WordPress or Tumblr. Add as much content as possible including videos.

Book Preview Feature

Would you like a preview of your book to appear on Goodreads? The previews, which are powered by the Kindle Cloud Reader, are possible now that Amazon owns Goodreads. Therefore, if your book isn't on Amazon, a preview won't appear for your book.

For an excerpt of your book to appear, follow these directions, which are from Goodreads:

1. Navigate to your author dashboard by clicking on your image in the top taskbar. The link is https://www.goodreads.com/author/dashboard.

2. Underneath the book in question, click "add preview."

3. Use the "Choose File" button to upload your ebook excerpt in PDF format. Your file should contain ONLY the excerpt of the book. If you add a PDF that contains your entire book, the entire book will be available on the site.

4. Choose which permissions you'd like to allow using the radio buttons (either "Members can only read this preview in their browsers" or "Members can read this preview in their browsers and download it").

5. Click "Upload File."

Note: I didn't follow the steps mentioned above, and yet a preview of my book was available on Goodreads. Before trying to add a preview, search for your book. If the word Preview appears beneath your book cover, you won't need to take any further actions. This feature appears to be another benefit to listing your book on Amazon.

You need to establish yourself as a Goodreads user before setting up your author dashboard. Once your dashboard is established, be sure to use all the features Goodreads offers to position yourself as best you can.

Goodreads as Part of Your Marketing Strategy

Your next step is to consider how you can incorporate Goodreads into your marketing. Start by following these steps:

1. Write the best book you can.

2. Demonstrate that you have a passion for reading. Read as many books as you can, and review and rate them.

3. Create bookshelves by genre to reveal your reading preferences. This way, you can build alliances with other readers who share your passion for the same genres, particularly if they write books in a particular genre you enjoy.

4. Respond to friend requests—accepting or denying according to your preferences—and follow whom you'd like to connect with. Note: The Goodreads friend limit is 5,000, similar to Facebook. However, you can have an unlimited number of fans and followers.

5. Join a reading group and become an active member.

6. Start a group. It could be a book group or a genre group or a group related to your nonfiction preferences, such as history.

7. Share your favorite books on social media.

8. Promote other authors you meet on Goodreads.

9. Take part in the Goodreads Choice Awards by voting for your favorite books.

10. Read, read, and read some more.

Writing the best book you can is vital to succeeding everywhere on the Internet. By writing a book that readers love, you may have an opportunity to be nominated for the Goodreads Choice Awards.

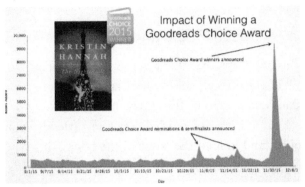

Market Your Book Carefully

There are a couple of Goodreads widgets to consider adding to your website. Here are two widgets that can be beneficial for authors:

- A Goodreads follow icon

- An icon that says "add my book to your shelf"

You'll find these widgets and icons by following these steps.

1. Click the arrow (drop-down menu) located to the right of your profile image on the taskbar.

2. Click Edit Profile.

3. Click Widgets on the Account Settings page.

If you use Blogger, follow Goodreads' advice on installing a widget:

1. Navigate to your Blogger dashboard.

2. Underneath Manage Blog, click Design.

3. Click "add a gadget" where you'd like the widget to appear.

4. A pop-up should appear. Scroll down to HTML / Javascript.

5.   Click the "+" next to it.

6.   Copy and paste the widget code into the box and save.

Social Media and Goodreads

Earlier in this book, you read that you can sync Goodreads to Facebook and have all of your Goodreads updates appear on your Facebook profile, but I don't endorse doing this. It's better to write a status update on Facebook about a book you finished, tag a few friends who have also read the book, and upload the cover of the book. This type of status update will generate far more engagement than a Goodreads auto-post to Facebook. This is also true for Twitter and any other social media networks you use.

For Pinterest, start a Goodreads pinboard and as you finish a book, pin images of the book covers with a sentence about why you liked or didn't like the book. Do the same on Instagram.

On Tumblr, upload the cover and add your complete review. Do the same thing on Google+. On LinkedIn, you can upload the image and create a blog post on LinkedIn's publishing platform, or you can write a one-sentence review and add your review as an update.

These are some of the ways you can incorporate Goodreads and your passion for reading into your social media marketing; but auto-posting directly from Goodreads— while it would save you time— won't generate the type of engagement you want nor will it represent your brand appropriately.

If you still want to sync Goodreads with your social media, follow these steps:

1.   Click your image on the Goodreads taskbar.

2.   Click Edit Profile.

3.   Click the tab Apps.

Your Facebook Author Page and Goodreads

Another way to incorporate Goodreads into your social media is to create a separate tab on your Facebook Author Page. Once you create the tab, your readers can open it and discover what you've read. Just follow these steps:

1. Go to your Goodreads author dashboard.

2. Scroll down to the section titled Facebook Page Tab.

3. Click the link in green. The link will say Add the Goodreads App. A pop-up will appear and ask you to select your Facebook Author Page.

4. Double-click the correct page (you may have more than one page) until a click appears. Then click Add Page Tab.

5. You'll then see a checkmark on your Goodreads author dashboard indicating that the connection was made.

FACEBOOK PAGE TAB

Display ratings and reviews for your books right on your Facebook Page.
preview »

1. Create a Facebook Page if you don't already have one.
2. Add the Goodreads App to your page.
    ✓ Added!

Then just visit your page and click the Goodreads logo (see screenshot at right; you may have to click the down arrow to reveal more tabs). Your author information should appear automatically!

6. When you navigate to your Facebook page, you'll find the books you wrote, your quotes, reviews by your readers, a list of your Goodreads groups, and a list of the books you've read. You can use your tab settings to adjust the information displayed.

How Nonfiction Authors Can Benefit from Goodreads

If you write nonfiction, you may be wondering how Goodreads can help you. Follow the steps I mentioned at the beginning of this document, and think about creating a group. And consider the success these two nonfiction authors attained on Goodreads:

- Holly Tucker started a group around her book *Blood Work: A Tale of Medicine & Murder in the Scientific Revolution*. At the time, she was a new author and didn't have many ratings. Therefore, Tucker created a group. As of January 2016, she had 1,630 ratings and 219 reviews. Those are great results for a new author.

- Charles Duhigg self-published *The Power of Habit*. He became so popular that he found a publisher and *The New York Times* featured his book. As of January 2016, he had 106,208 ratings and 6,505 reviews.

How to Add Images, Quotes, Updates, and Blog Posts

Adding a Comment and Image in a Group
Do you belong to a group on Goodreads? If you do, and you should, you can leave a comment as well as add an image with your comment. This is how:

- Once you are in the discussion thread, go to the comment box.

- Click the "add book/author" link above the comment box.

- In the popup, select Book or Author. If you want to add the book cover, type the title of the book. If you want to add an image of the author, type his or her name. Indicate whether you want to add the image or add a link that will generate the image.

- If you want to add an image that's not a book cover, then you need to source the image online by typing the URL from the web page where the image appears.

Step One

comment   add book/author   (some html is ok)

Add your comment here.

Post   (preview)

11979 characters left
☑ Add to my Update Feed
☐ Notify me when people reply

Step Two

Add a reference:

Book   **Author**

Book   search

Search for a book to add a reference

add: ○ link   ◉ cover

Add an Update About What You're Reading

On your home page you can add an update about what you are reading. Here's how:

1. Navigate to the Home tab.

2. Under Currently Reading, click Update Status, Add a New Book, or Add a General Update.

Step One

CURRENTLY READING

Business For Authors. How To Be An Author
updated Jan 05, 2016 05:37AM   update status

add a new book   add a general update

Step Two

CURRENTLY READING

Business For Authors. How To Be An Author
updated Jan 05, 2016 05:37AM   update status

I'm on page 0   of 310. -or- I'm finished!

```
                                                        /
```

[Save Progress]   Cancel

add a new book   add a general update

What are you currently reading?

Start typing the name of a book...

Do You Have a Blog? Add Your Posts to Goodreads

Just follow these directions:

1. Navigate to your author dashboard by clicking your avatar.

2. Under the section titled "Your Blog," click "Write a new post."

YOUR BLOG

Your blog stats: 4 posts | 161 followers

Blog post: Marketing Advice from a Publishing Pro: Jane Friedman Shares Her Best Tips (published Sep 02, 2014 05:02PM)
Stats: 78 views, 0 comments

Blog post: 56 Social Media Terms Writers Need to Know (published May 19, 2014 10:06AM)
Stats: 29 views, 0 comments

Blog post: What I've Learned about Amazon and Social Media Marketing (published Dec 11, 2013 11:13AM)
Stats: 47 views, 0 comments, 1 person liked this

View your blog | Write a new post

Add Quotes

Readers love quotes from great books and about the joy of reading. Just follow these steps to start adding some:

*   Click the arrow to the right of the Explore tab.

*   A dropdown menu will appear.

*   Click quotes.

*   Add a quote either by typing in an author's name or clicking the Add A Quote link.

Step One

ɔns   **Explore**   ▾

Genres
Listopia
Giveaways
Choice Awards
Popular
Goodreads Voice
Ebooks

Fun
Trivia
Quizzes
Quotes

Community
Creative Writing
People
Events

Step Two

Popular Quotes

Find quotes by keyword, author

| Search |

My Quotes | Add A Quote

Step Three

Quotes > Add

Before adding a new quote please first do a search and make sure it doesn't already exist in the database.

quote (No need for quotation marks)

author (Start typing for auto-complete. Only put the name please)

tags (Comma separated: inspirational, science, humor, etc)

| **Save** | cancel

Host Giveaways of Your Books

Contests are easy to create and run on Goodreads because Goodreads is a partner in the endeavor. Follow these steps:

1. Navigate to the arrow next to Explore, click it, and select Giveaways. On the right column, you'll find a green link that says List a Giveaway.

2. You will then arrive at a page asking for details about your book giveaway, such as the start and finish dates for your promotion, ISBN or book ID, the number of copies you'll give away, genre, contact information, and a few more details.

3. You can give away hard copies or ebooks.

4. Agree to the Goodreads terms and click Save. Goodreads should review and approve your giveaway in about two days.

5. Goodreads will notify you of the winners and provide their names and addresses. You can add a bookmark with the book and a note that says you hope the winners enjoy reading your book. However, you can't ask them to take any actions, such as writing a review on Amazon or joining your email list. Goodreads strictly prohibits marketing to the giveaway winners.

Step One

Genres

Listopia

Giveaways

Choic~ ^~~~~~
Free book give.
Popular

Goodreads Voice

Ebooks

Fun

Trivia

Quizzes

Quotes

Community

Creative Writing

People

Events

Step Two

Giveaways

Be the first to read new books! Prerelease books are listed for giveaway by publishers and authors, and members can enter to win. Winners are picked randomly at the end of the giveaway.

Previous Winners

List a Giveaway

Giveaways You've Entered

Giveaway Terms

Step Three

List Your Giveaway: Enter Details

Complete the form below and read the terms and conditions to start building buzz for your book! Please note winning members are encouraged but not required to write a review of the book they receive. All user entries are subject to the Giveaway Terms and Conditions.

Giveaway Details

Start date ?   2016 ⬍   March ⬍   1 ⬍

End date ?   2016 ⬍   March ⬍   9 ⬍

Book release date   ⬍   ⬍   ⬍

ISBN/ISBN13 ?   [_____]   Switch to Book ID

Eligible countries ?

> United States
> Canada
> United Kingdom
> Australia

CTRL-click to select multiple countries (CMD-click on a Mac)

Number of copies   [____]

Book contains mature content ?   ☐

Giveaway description ?

> Example: Enter for a chance to win one of 100 advance/signed/first edition copies of [Title] by [Author]! (include a brief description of the book if you'd like).

HTML is disallowed   1500 character limit

Primary genre   [_____ ⬍]

Secondary genre (optional)   [_____ ⬍]

Contact information ?

> Name, Email Address, Affiliation with Giveaway Book

☐ I have read and agree to the giveaway listing terms and conditions. (You must open the link to continue)

Book Giveaway Best Practices

1. You can give your book away at any time. Goodreads recommends setting up your giveaway six weeks before your book is published. This is sound advice.

2. How many books can you afford to give away? Goodreads' data indicates that a 20-copy giveaway will attract 940 entries in the United States.

3. Your giveaway needs to run for a month to get the maximum exposure.

4. Don't ignore Goodreads's email verification. Your giveaway won't start until Goodreads approves of your giveaway and you formally agree to the terms.

5. Use your social media and email list to promote your giveaway. You can also purchase a self-serve ad on Goodreads to aid the promotion.

6. Goodreads will notify you of the winners and your addresses.

It's important to note that Goodreads doesn't allow any promotion to a giveaway's winners and doesn't require the winners to write reviews.

Goodreads Deals

On May 17, 2016, Goodreads announced the launch of its Goodreads Deals program.

This is how Goodreads described the program: "Goodreads Deals is a feature that connects Goodreads members with noteworthy discounts on titles they've expressed an interest in. We send you an email when there's a great ebook deal on a book you've placed on your Want to Read shelf or by an Author You Follow. We also offer Deals by Genre for Bestseller, Mystery & Thrillers, Romance, and Fantasy & Science Fiction."

So far this program is in beta form. Also, it's restricted to the genres listed above.

Goodreads plans to include the Kindle Store, Apple iBooks, Barnes & Noble Nook, Google Play, and Kobo. The program will launch in the U.S. and then spread to other areas of the globe.

What's wonderful about the Deals program is that you'll reach more people who have never read your books before. Because whenever anyone adds books to their want-to-read bookshelf, Goodreads will send that user an email about the promotion even if that reader hadn't read any books by that author in the past.

To learn more about Goodreads Deals and signup, use this link: https://www.goodreads.com/deals/about

Once you sign up, you'll be taken to a landing page where you can select your favorite genres.

Congratulations!

You're all signed up for Goodreads Deals.
Please take a moment to review your settings.

Deals

☑ Deals from my Want to Read shelf
Email me deals for ebooks on my Want to Read shelf.

☑ Deals for my authors
Email me deals for ebooks by authors I follow.

☑ Deals by genre
Email me daily deals for ebooks in the following genres:

☑ Bestsellers

☑ Romance

☑ Mystery & Thrillers

☑ Fantasy & Science Fiction

Retailers

Send me deals available at the following ebook retailers:

☑ Amazon Kindle

☑ Apple iBooks

☑ Barnes & Noble Nook

☑ Google Play

☑ Kobo

Save

Goodreads Home

I think that the union between Amazon and Goodreads is finally working and authors and readers are in line to reap the benefits of some innovative changes.

Become a Joiner

Demonstrate your love of reading and discussing books by joining a book group. Here's how to find and join groups:

1.   Navigate to the Groups tab on Goodreads.

2.   Search for a group by title or description.

3.   Consider starting a group.

4.   Browse groups by tag (keyword.)

This screenshot shows you how to search for a group or start one.

Groups

Find Groups by Title or Description   Search   Create a Group

On the right column, you can browse groups by tag.

BROWSE BY TAG

bookclub (7239)	horror (808)
fantasy (4435)	writing (739)
romance (3383)	reading (684)
roleplay (2393)	role-play (676)
fiction (2253)	adventure (658)
young-adult (2055)	sci-fi (630)
books (1906)	thriller (599)
fun (1832)	authors (589)
book-club (1750)	historical-fiction (563)
rp (1442)	love (543)
science-fiction (1265)	history (532)
ya (1031)	bookclub-any-type-of-
mystery (945)	book (528)
paranormal (877)	friends (515)
literature (831)	non-fiction (509)
	paranormal-romance (493)

More...

Participate in Goodreads groups the same way you would a LinkedIn group.

1. Don't self-promote.

2. Be an active member.

3. Respond to comments.

4. Initiate discussion threads.

Goodreads is first and foremost a social media network for readers. However, following the steps noted in this document, you can incorporate Goodreads into your marketing strategy and promote your passion for reading.

Chapter 17
Be a Gutsy Blogger
and Find Your Niche & Voice

Blogging is to writing what extreme sports are to athletics:
more free-form, more accident-prone, less formal, more alive.
It is, in many ways, writing out loud.
Andrew Sullivan

Are you new to blogging? Are you disappointed by how little traffic your blog generates?

Would you like information on how to explore opportunities to join a blogging community? Keep reading.

Lessons from Nora Ephron

Remember Nora Ephron? She was a gutsy, funny, successful, and a creative writer. She wrote the screenplays *You've Got Mail, Silkwood, Sleepless in Seattle, and Heartburn.*

Huh, you ask? Yeah, they probably hit the big screen before you were born so if you need to know anything about Ephron it's this: she did things her way.

Now there's a lesson for blogging.

She wasn't interested in mimicking someone else; she wanted to be different and distinguish herself. An incredibly creative woman, Ephron was fearless in her honesty and possessed a killer sense of humor.

She used her gifts and talent to distinguish herself in the writing world and Hollywood. In many ways, this quote from her screenplay Heartburn epitomizes her life: "And then the dreams break into a million tiny pieces. The dream dies. Which leaves you with a choice: you can settle for reality, or you can go off, like a fool, and dream another dream."

If you write historical novels, be the best in your genre. If you focus on rescued animals, do whatever it takes to be the best source for tips on finding and adopting rescued cats and puppies. If you are a food blogger, create your niche in gluten-free, Tuscan, or holiday cooking. Discover your talent, pursue it, and brand it.

To be a great blogger, you must develop your own voice and style, and stick to it. Ephron spiced her posts with insight, pithy humor, and self-reflection. She wasn't afraid to admit what she didn't understand or confess what she didn't believe, despite someone's expert opinion.

She knew how to help us smile and even chuckle while being informed. Her blog was at times as irreverent as the fake orgasm scene in *When Harry Met Sally*, and that's why we adored her and loved her blog, screenplays, and books.

4 Keys to Blogging Success

Some bloggers do extremely well while others limp along. The key to having a successful blog is simple:

- Provide the best content you can.
- Create content readers want.
- Optimize your blog with keywords.
- Use social media to alert others of your latest musings.

These four concepts are essential to generating traffic to your blog. While the advice seems simple, maintaining a successful blog is not. Providing stellar content every week for your readers takes a lot of work. It also takes commitment. Then, to convert your blog readers into people who purchase your books takes patience and active engagement.

Don't become discouraged. Despite the hurdles, blogging is a very effective way to be discovered on the Internet, to keep your website updated, to improve your search engine ranking, and to help you sell books.

It can also be a lot of fun.

Audience, Audience, Audience

A marketer's first question to you will be: Who is your audience? Whom are you writing for?

A common mistake writers make is to write for other writers—for colleagues who encourage them, root for them, and share their experiences, frustrations and successes. Or, they write for themselves.

Instead, write for your readers and prospective fans. As you type those first few words, think about one person who buys your books or who looks to your poetry for inspiration. What would that person want to read next? Does that reader want to be entertained or informed? Always write for your readers and create the content they need to read, they long to read.

Tease Readers with Keyword-Rich Blog Titles

Blog titles need to attract attention, have zing, and appeal to a reader's curiosity.

Think about the teasers at the top of newspapers. Their purpose is to entice you to drop some coins into newspaper racks and read the stories below the fold and on the newspaper's internal pages. The next time you write a title for your blog, try to write teaser copy. Use words that will lure your readers in.

- Use Google Adwords to find keywords particular to your niche, and use them in your title and in the post. Use "long-tailed" keywords, terms that include two or more words that are unique.

- Use numbers in your blog title. People are more likely to click on a title if it contains numbers—especially odd numbers. Would you be able to resist this title: "5 Ways to Master Facebook"? Isn't it tempting to click on that link to find out how you can master Facebook in just five steps?

- Make sure your title is eight words or less. Again, think about the teasers above the masthead and try to mimic them. The next time you're at a checkout stand at your grocery store, scan the tabloids for teaser copy.

- Write your blog title after you write your newest post. Writing can sometimes take you to a different destination than you planned. Flow with the words, let them take you wherever they may, and write your title last.

- Avoid titles that appear catchy to you, yet convey no meaning to a wider audience. For example, instead of using the blog title "On Your Mark, Get Set, Tweet!" use this one: "5 Reasons Every Writer Needs to Use Twitter."

- Analyze your headline. I like to use the Advanced Marketing Institute's test for analyzing blog headlines. Strive to attain a score of at least 30% and ideally 50%.

6 Tips for Finding Your Blogging Voice

It's important for you to develop your unique voice. In fact, it's imperative. Here are some suggestions.

1. Be original.

2. Imagine you're writing for one person. Write a detailed page about that reader, including age, gender, reading and drink preferences, etc. (I wish mine would like martinis, but I suspect she would rather spit out a martini than swallow one.)

3. Read your post out loud. Does it sound like you?

4. Write about what you're passionate about.

5. Mix it up until you find your groove.

6. Always be honest.

18 Blogging Tips to Get You Started

Here are some thoughts and suggestions on how to be successful in your endeavor as a blogger.

1. Use great photos that quickly convey the message of your posts. If possible, use more than one photo to break up the text and offer the eye a break from stacks of black text.

2. Be consistent in your posting. Was it your plan to post twice a week, but now you only post once a month? Decide how often you can reasonably create captivating posts and keep to your schedule. Having said that, strive to write one new post every week.

3. Some bloggers write four or more posts in one sitting, post them online, and schedule them to publish at a later date. If it's easier to write several in a row, do it.

4. Develop your blogging voice. Look at copyblogger.com to get a sense of the writing style of that well-known blog. Be enthusiastic in your writing, demonstrate a bit of flair, and nurture the voice that best suits you.

5. Promote your blog on every social media network you join.

6. Get to know your readers by responding to their comments on your blog.

7. If your readers have blogs, take time to read some of their posts and leave a comment if you feel so moved.

8. Did one of your readers ask a question in her comments? Great! You have a topic for your next blog post.

9. Do you have an avid reader who always leaves articulate comments? Ask him to write a guest post.

10. Do you teach writing and revision workshops? Sponsor a contest and offer the winner free admission to your next workshop or free editing services for the first chapter of a book.

11. Always end your blogs with a question to elicit feedback.

12. Join Triberr and send a Triberr request to your most loyal fans. They will appreciate the new exposure their tweets receive.

13. Use your editorial calendar to capture all those great, fleeting ideas you have for future posts.

14. Include common and uncommon holidays in your calendar so you can occasionally spin a post around one. For example, "5 Ways to Put the Fireworks Back in Your Writing."

15. Have you noticed that other bloggers follow the exact same outline every time they write? Establish a style for your blog.

16. Remember to use social share icons to encourage sharing your post on social media.

17. Make an appointment with your keyboard. Calendar your writing time and stick to it.

18. Provide an opportunity for readers to subscribe to your blog via email.

If you have any questions about blogging, be sure to send me a tweet at @CaballoFrances.

Resources

Password Cheat Sheet

When you select your password, make sure it's impossible to crack. Use lowercase and uppercase letters, numbers, and symbols such as ^ or #. Do not use the word "password" in your login; there are 10 million people who already use it, so it's easy for hackers to crack.

Here's an easy system for creating passwords:

1. Write down the names of your two favorite authors.

2. Use the first three letters of one of the author's last names, and use them to start your password. Let's say you selected Hemingway. The first part of your password would be **Hem.**

3. Select three or more numbers. Don't use 123. Mix the numbers up.

4. Use the first three letters of the second author's last name. Let's say it's Allende. So far your password might be **Hem982All.**

5. Add symbols to the mix. Your final password might be **Hem9*82All@** or **Hem982All*@.**

6. As you add social media networks, change one variable. Now you'll have a unique password for each social media network you use.

Profile and Image Dimensions Cheat Sheet

Here are the dimensions you need to know (all measurements are in pixels and are denoted as wide x high):

- Facebook: 180 × 180 pixels
- LinkedIn: 200 × 200 pixels and 500 × 500 pixels
- Twitter: 400 × 400 pixels and displays at 200 × 200 pixels
- Pinterest: 165 × 165 pixels
- Goodreads adopts the profile image from the social media network you use to sign up. Book covers should be 150 × 245 pixels, and the file format must be either .jpg or .gif.

Now let's look at the header/banner dimensions you need to know right now (all measurements are in pixels and are denoted as wide × high):

- Facebook: Minimum of 828 × 315. Make sure it's a JPEG or PNG.
- Twitter: 1500 × 500.
- LinkedIn: 1400 × 425.
- Pinterest doesn't have one.
- Goodreads doesn't have one.

Social Media Post Idea Cheat Sheet

1. Inspirational quotes

2. Fun quotes

3. Fun, personal items that your readers would enjoy reading

4. Famous author quotes

5. Quotes about reading, books, libraries

6. Images of unusual bookshelves

7. Images of beautiful libraries

8. Images of unusual bookstores

9. Interesting stories about famous authors, including the number of times publishers rejected their manuscripts

10. Polls

11. Statistics or data

12. Questions

13. Branded images

14. Infographics, if you are a nonfiction author

15. Tips, if you are a nonfiction author

16. Recommendations of books you love (use the hashtag #FridayReads on Twitter when you do this)

17. Requests for advice

18. TBT: Throwback Thursday images

19. Memes

20. Testimonials for your book

21. Contests

22. Videos

23. Controversial questions

Twitter Do and Don't Checklist

Even if you're a fairly seasoned Twitter user, it might be a good idea to review some of these faux pas. Why? They may be preventing you from attracting more readers, book reviewers, and book bloggers from following you. Use this easy Do and Don't checklist to make sure your tweets are done right.

- Don't use all 140 characters available to you when you tweet. Instead, keep your tweets to between 110 and 120 characters. Using fewer than 140 characters will give others a chance to retweet you without having to reconfigure your message. And there will be room for your username to credit you as the author of the content.

- Are you #doing #this #with #your #hashtags in your #tweets? Refrain from using more than two hashtags because the more hashtags you use, the fewer retweets you'll receive.

- Are you interacting with other authors? If you're not, you're missing a huge opportunity to collaborate and co-market books and blogs. It's important to be friendly on Twitter, meet other authors—including those who write in your genre (perhaps **especially** those authors)—and promote other authors. The more authors you meet and promote, the more they will suggest your books to their readers.

- Never retweet tweets that praise you or your book. I once read somewhere that retweeting tweets of praise is like laughing at your own jokes—when the jokes aren't even funny. Promoting yourself in this manner is akin to bragging.

- Are you ignoring the 80/20 rule? Guess what? Social media, including Twitter, isn't about you. It's not even about your book, poetry, blog, or website. Social media is about engagement first and content second. Make sure that 80 percent of your content comes from a variety of sources and that you restrict your own content to only 20 percent of your tweets.

- Are you responding to replies or questions? If not, you're missing an opportunity to engage with your readers and colleagues. Engaging with other users is the single most important aspect of social media. Don't neglect this important activity.

- Are you tweeting only between 9 a.m. and 5 p.m.? No one expects your account to be a 24/7 operation, but your followers don't log off when you start preparing dinner. You are tweeting to a worldwide audience, so schedule some tweets early and some late.

- How often are you tweeting? Tweeting too often can be problematic for your followers. There's no set formula for how often you should be tweeting. However, unless you're the most interesting person in the world, chances are if you're clogging up their timelines, they'll get turned off in a hurry. Space your tweets at least two hours apart.

- Use caution when punctuating your tweets with exclamation points and capital letters. You wouldn't yell at your readers in person, so don't do it on Twitter. (Capital letters in emails are considered shouting language. Some also feel that way about words written completely in capital letters on social media.) Use exclamation points sparingly and when in doubt, one is enough. Or skip them entirely.

Next Steps

Ready to continue learning more about social media?
Sign up for my free email social media course
and receive a bonus ebook at
www.SocialMediaJustforWriters.com.

If you enjoyed this book, please leave a review.

About the Author

Frances Caballo is an author and social media strategist and manager for writers. She's a regular speaker at the San Francisco Writers Conference and a contributing writer at Joel Friedlander's blog, TheBookDesigner.com. In addition, she's the Social Media Expert and blogger for BookWorks and a regular blogger at Bowker's Self-Published Author. She's written numerous social media books for authors including *The Author's Guide to Goodreads, Social Media in 30 Minutes a Day, Blogging Just for Writers,* and *Avoid Social Media Time Suck.* Her focus is on helping authors surmount the barriers that keep them from flourishing online, building their platform, finding new readers, and selling more books. Her clients include authors of every genre and writer's conferences.

Made in the USA
Middletown, DE
19 December 2019

81336503R00129